DANTE'S COMEDY

1. *THE INFERNO*

Translated by Nicholas Kilmer
Illustrated by Benjamin Martinez

BRANDEN PUBLISHING CO. 1985

Library of Congress Cataloging in Publication Data
Dante Alighieri, 1265-1321.
Dante's comedy.

Translation of: Divina commedia.
Includes index.
Contents: 1. The Inferno.
I. Kilmer, Nicholas. II. Title.
PQ4315.K55 1985 851'.1 85-3816
ISBN 0-8283-1884-0 (pbk. : v. 1)
ISBN 0-937832-28-6

Cloth edition published by Dante University of America Press
by arrangement with Branden Publishing company.

BRANDEN PUBLISHING COMPANY
PO Box 843
17 Station Street
Brookline Village, MA 02147

THE INFERNO

The Dante University of America Foundation
acknowledges, with gratitude, a donation
from Francesco Correra, Michele Correra, and
Elizabeth Correra Harrell, in honor
of the courage and graciousness of their parents,
Domenico Correra and Giuseppina DiVicenzo Correra.

Contents

The Fourth Level

7. The fourth level is guarded by Plutus. Here misers and squanderers are punished. Virgil explains the role of Fortune in the distribution of the world's wealth. The poets enter the fifth level, the marsh of Styx, where the wrathful and sullen are.

The Fifth Level

8. Flegias ferries the poets across the Styx in his boat, and brings them to the gates of the city of Dis. During the crossing Dante converses with Filippo Argenti.

The Sixth Level (City of Dis)

9. Demons prevent the poets from entering the city of Dis until a messenger specially sent from heaven subdues them. Within the walls, heretics are punished in flaming tombs.

10. Dante converses with the heretics Farinata and Cavalcante de' Cavalcanti, the father of his friend, the poet Guido Cavalcanti.

11. Virgil explains the plan of hell, and its stratification according to the relative degrees of evil that attach to different sins.

The Seventh Level

12. The seventh level, that of the violent, is presided over by the Minotaur, and is divided into three rings. In the first — a river of boiling blood watched by armed centaurs — are punished the spirits of those who were violent against their neighbors' persons or property.

13. The second ring is a woods in which the spirits of suicides (those violent against their own persons) have been transformed to trees; those wasteful of their own possessions are torn apart by dogs.

14. The third ring is a burning desert where showers of fire fall on those violent against God (blasphemers) and those who violate nature and nature's bounty (sodomites and usurers.) Virgil explains the source of the rivers of hell.

15. Still in the third ring, Dante converses with his former teacher, Brunetto Latini, who is amongst the sodomites.

16. Still in the third ring, after Dante has spoken with three sodomites from Florence, the poets come to the edge of the desert, a steep cliff downward.

17. Virgil brings the monster Geryon up from the abyss, and, after Dante has conversed with a group of usurers, the poets mount Geryon, and the monster descends again.

The Eighth Level (Malebolge)

18. The eighth level is divided into ten trenches. In this level are punished those guilty of fraud (or malicious deceit), segregated as appropriate according to specific sins within this broad classification. In the first trench are pimps and seducers, among whom Dante speaks to Venedico Caccianemico and Jason. They cross this trench by a natural bridge and look into the second trench, where flatterers are punished.

19. The third trench contains simoniacs, clergy who have sold the church's offices. Dante speaks with Pope Nicholas III, and learns that Boniface VIII and Clement V are expected in their turn.

20. The fourth trench contains witches and soothsayers. Virgil shows Dante the witch Manto, and recounts her founding of Mantua, Virgil's native city.

21. The fifth trench contains those guilty of corruption in public office (barratry or graft). Dante and Virgil witness the spirit of such a sinner being thrown by a demon into the trench. A group of demons is commissioned to guide the poets to the next crossing.

22. Dante converses with one of those guilty of corruption in public office, and the spirit's escape from the demons occasions a quarrel, which allows the poets to escape their company.

23. Finding no bridge to cross the sixth trench, the poets descend into it and, for a time, walk in company with the hypocrites who are punished there. (Annas and Caiaphas, who advised the execution of Jesus, are among these.) The poets ascend the bank that overlooks the next trench.

24. The seventh trench contains thieves, conspicuous among whom is Vanni Fucci, who robbed the sacristy of a Florentine church.

25. Still in the seventh trench, Dante observes the metamorphic punishments of five thieves from Florence.

26. The eighth trench contains those who gave maliciously deceitful advice, or who advised deceit. Among them Dante encounters Diomedes; and Ulysses, who recounts his last voyage to the Antipodes.

27. Still in the eighth trench, Dante speaks to Guido Montefeltro, a corrupt adviser.

28. The ninth trench contains those who instigated schism, and scandal. Dante speaks with Mohammed, and with three others who fomented schism.

29. The tenth trench contains those who engineer falsehood — impersonators, liars, forgers, alchemists. The poets talk with two alchemists.

30. Still in the tenth trench, Dante observes the spirits of two impersonators, and is spectator of an argument between Master Adam, a counterfeiter, and Sinon, a perjurer.

31. At the inner limit of the tenth trench, the poets come upon giants who are condemned to stay there, and one of whom, Antaeus, lowers them down to the ninth level.

The Ninth Level (Cocytus)

32. The ninth level is Cocytus, a frozen lake, where traitors are punished. In the area known as Caina, Dante encounters those who betrayed their own kin.

33. In the area known as Antenora are those who betrayed their countries. Among them Dante finds the traitor Ugolino, and hears from him the story of his betrayal by Archbishop Ruggieri. In the next area, Ptolomaea, are those who betrayed their guests.

34. The poets reach the central pit of hell, Judecca, which contains those who betrayed their legitimate superiors. Here Satan is imprisoned; and, in his three mouths, he devours, eternally, the traitors Judas, Brutus, and Cassius. Virgil, with Dante on his back, escapes hell by climbing down the fur of Satan; and the poets, having passed the earth's center, again emerge in the open.

Introduction

Our reading of Dante's *Comedy* is affected by what has accrued to the work during the seven centuries since it was composed. Translation and illustration are a form of reading. Dante has entered the knowledge of English-speaking readers much colored by the Romantic imagery and sentiment to be found in nineteenth-century interpretations.

In preparing this edition, the illustrator and translator worked independently, from Dante's text, endeavoring to find a mode of presentation that was close to Dante's vision, while keeping respect for the cultural expectations of our own audience.

We hope this book can be read for pleasure, as a long poem should be read.

Dante called his great work *The Comedy* — signifying a narrative with a happy ending. The narrative is about the journey of the human spirit through trial, and toward salvation. The journey takes place in three segments of which this, "The Inferno," is the first.

Like all travel literature, the tale recounts things that are unusual, fantastic, and sometimes difficult to credit.

Although he may see and describe it differently, Dante walks in the same world we do. Like ours, his responses vary through a wide range that includes the humor of an optimist who is, sometimes, held at bay by adversity.

Both the illustration and translation mean to be as lucid, as varied, and as straightfoward as fidelity to Dante's original text requires. Where, occasionally, the translation steps aside from a literal rendition, the intent is to incorporate hints of the explanatory material Dante could assume his readers possessed in their own experience.

1

Halfway on the path our life is
I found I was in a dark woods;
for I had lost my direction.

It is so much to speak: how hard
this wilderness — rough, harsh enough
remembering it makes me afraid.

Death can hardly be more strenuous;
but I will speak what I have seen,
to show what I found of the good.

Not good at saying how I got there,
for I was somnolent at the time
I abandoned the true path,

I did find myself at a hill's foot
there, where the valley that oppressed
my heart with fear, came to an end.

I saw, looking up to its height,
its crest clothed with that planet's light
who leads us right, whatever our path.

So my fear was somewhat comforted —
a liquid suffering my heart
endured in the long night I'd passed.

It was like being breathless
fresh beached on the bank of the sea
gaping back at the dangerous water.

My spirit, still fugitive,
turned, looked back over the pass
that before let pass no one living.

I lay my tired body down briefly,
then journeyed up the barren hill
keeping my strong right foot lowest.

And almost at the gradient's start,
a quick and subtle leopard, clothed
in its spotted pelt: I saw this;

nor would it leave my vision,
rather so blocked my path
that often I turned to go back.

It was the dawn of the morning,
the sun rising with the very stars
that were with it when divine love

moved these lovely objects the first time.
So there was cause to hope for good
of this wild beast in its gay hide:

hope of dawn and the spring season —
yet not sufficient to quell fear
at vision of lion appearing.

Head high, ravenous with hunger
so great the air throbbed with it, it seemed
the lion advanced against me;

and a wolf whose lean carcase looked
to incorporate all cravings.
She's made many people's lives mean.

In response to her demeanor,
the fear of her so burdened me
I lost hope I'd reach the highland.

Like someone who wishes to win
and, comes the moment of losing,
turns with tears of self-rebuking;

this beast had such an effect on me;
advancing without peace, forced me
back, back, into the sun's absence.

While I hurtled down toward ruin
the vision was offered to me
of one whom long silence made hoarse.

When I saw him in the great waste
I called him, "Take pity on me
whoever you are, ghost or real man."

"No man," he answered, "but once man.
My parents were Lombards, and both
were citizens of Mantua.

Born late in Julius Caesar's time,
I lived in Rome under good Augustus
in the time of false, lying gods.

I was a poet; sang the just
son of Anchises. He left Troy,
his splendid nation, in ashes.

Why, then, revisit your ruins?
not scale the delightful mountain
that's the source and cause of all joy?"

"You are Virgil, then? The live spring,
source of such river of language?"
I answered, blushing with shyness.

"Honor, example to all poets,
may the great love that brought me to search
into your words, assist me now.

You are my teacher, my author.
Only from you have I drawn out
the fine style I am acclaimed for.

Look at the beast that turned me back.
Your wisdom's tried. Help me with her.
She makes the pulse in my veins shake."

"A different track would suit you,"
he said, seeing me crying there,
"if you're to escape this wilderness.

The beast that is making you cry
lets no one pass by her pathway,
but burdens them down till they die.

Her nature's so guilty, vicious,
she can't fill her greedy craving.
After she feeds, she's hungrier.

Many the beasts to whom she's paired;
there will be more, till the greyhound
comes to put her to death in pain.

Nourished not on earth or metal,
but on wisdom, love, uprightness,
his nation is between the felts.

He will save dishonoured Italy,
for which Camilla died of wounds;
and Turnus, Euryalus, Nisus...

He'll hound the wolf through every city
till he drives her to hell again,
from which envy first released her.

Therefore I think it best for you
that you follow me — I be guide
to draw you through eternal space.

There you will hear screams of despair,
will see ancient spirits suffering,
each wailing in the second death.

After, you'll see others in fire,
who are content; for they hope to come
among the blessed at some time.

If you wish to rise to the blessed,
I will leave you to a worthier
spirit guide, when I leave you.

For the king who reigns from that place,
since I rebelled against his laws,
wills I not enter his city.

He orders throughout; rules from there
where his city and high seat are.
Those he chooses are the happy ones."

I said to him, "Poet, I beg
by the God whom you did not know:
so I escape this and worse evil,

that you lead me through where you've said.
Then I will see St. Peter's gate,
after the ones you say are suffering."

He started and I followed him.

2

The day waned and the sky darkened,
taking the animals of earth
from their burdens. I, one, alone

prepared to sustain the hardship
of journey and of compassion
the mind must represent, unerring.

Muses, help me; high skill assist.
My memory took what I saw.
Let its worth show in the writing.

I began, "Poet, and my guide,
consider my strength and stamina
before trusting me to this hard path.

You said Aeneas, even live,
corruptible still in body,
sensible: walked the immortal world.

But if evil's adversary
allowed him, thought his purpose worthy,
as was himself, and what came of it;

it seems right to a thoughtful person.
For the heavens had chosen him
to father Rome and its empire,

which, to speak truth, he established
to consecrate the environs
where great Peter's successor sits.

In the journey you celebrate
he learned what made him fit for conquest;
a foundation for papal power.

Later Paul, the chosen vessel,
traveled there to confirm the faith,
source of our road to salvation.

But by whose leave can I go there?
I'm neither Aeneas nor Paul.
No one, nor I, thinks me worthy.

If I commit myself to this journey
I'm afraid to arrive a fool.
Be wise. Hear what I'm not saying well."

This was me disavowing my vow,
shifting purpose with the new thought
that stops the task at its inception.

On the dark hill I behaved this way:
thinking of it devoured the venture
I had entered into so quickly.

"If I have heard you correctly,"
the generous ghost answered me,
"Your spirit is lamed by cowardice,

frequently burdensome to people
so they shy from worthy projects:
beasts, at dusk, starting from false visions.

Let me resolve this dread of yours,
tell why I came, and what I heard
the moment I took pity on you.

I was with those held in suspension.
A lady called — so lovely, blessed,
that I asked to do her bidding.

Her eyes shone more than the stars do.
She started to speak gently, softly,
in angel's voice, in her own tongue:

'Courteous spirit of Mantua,
whose reputation lasts in the world,
and will survive as long as time;

a friend of mine — not fortune's friend —
is blocked on a wilderness slope;
has turned back on his road, for fear.

From what I hear of him in heaven,
I fear he's already so lost
I am late rising to assist him.

Go help him with your careful speech,
with the craft his safety requires,
so that I may be comforted.

I am Beatrice, who send you.
Love moved, and makes me speak. I come
from love; desire to return there.

When I'm before my lord again,
I will praise you before him often.'
She became silent. I replied,

'Lady of holy strength, in whom
the human race excells what's now
closed in the sublunary world,

so pleasing is your command, late
were it obeyed, were it followed now.
It is enough to say what you need.

Tell me, why are you not afraid
to come into this deep center,
leave broad space you long to return to?'

'I'll tell you briefly,' she answered,
'since you wish to understand fully,
why I don't fear entering here.

Only what has power to harm
need be feared. Other things having
no such power, need not be feared.

God, in his grace, has made me such
that your pain does not reach to me,
nor the flame of this burning place.

Heaven's lady's kind, and so deplores
what impedes him to whom I send you
she softens high judgement's harshness.

She called a request to Lucy:
"Your faithful man has need of you.
I deliver him to your care."

Lucy, champion against all pain,
rose, came to where I was sitting
conversing with aged Rachel.

She said, "Beatrice, God's true praise,
why not help him who so loved you
he forsook the crowd for your sake?

Don't you hear the call of his pain?
Not see the engulfing flood of death,
greater than sea, he's struggling with?"

Humans on earth were never quicker
to seek profit, flee what hurts them,
than I was when these words were spoken,

to come down from my blessed rest
trusting your modesty of speech,
which honors you, and those who hear you.' 12

After she'd spoken this to me
she turned, her eyes bright with weeping,
making me come still more quickly.

So I've come as she asked, freed you
of the wild beast who took from you
the short road to the crest of good.

And now, why are you hanging back?
Why entertain such meanness of heart?
Why be without zeal, or candor,

while three ladies of such holiness
in heaven's court look after you?
My words promise you so much good!"

Flowers droop, close, in the night's chill;
then, when the sun dawns over them,
rise up on their stems, all open.

So my exhausted courage did
and such good zeal flowed through my heart
that I spoke like a person set free:

"It is her compassion saves me;
your courtesy, who quickly heard
the true speech she delivered.

Your words have so inclined my heart
with desire for the journey,
I return to my old intention.

Now we'll go with a single will,
you the guide, the lord, and teacher."
This I said. He commenced walking.

I entered the deep wilderness path.

3

"This way to the city of grief.
This way to eternal pain.
This way to the lost people.

Justice inspired my great maker.
Divine power created me:
height of wisdom: primary love.

Before me were no things created,
but eternal; I am eternal.
Leave all hope when you enter."

I saw these words written in dark letters
over a gateway, and I asked,
"Teacher, their meaning is threatening..."

He answered me as an adept,
"You must drop all your distrust,
dispell all meanness of spirit.

We have come to where I told you
you would see the unhappy people
who've lost the use of their intellects."

And then he took me by the hand
with cheerful face, comforting me;
took me inside to what was hidden.

Sighs, groanings and shrieks of sorrow
sounded in a sky without stars,
so at the beginning I cried.

Varied tongues, awful languages,
words of hurt, the stress of anger,
high and hoarse voices, beating hands,

made uproar, like a great whirling
in air eternally stained dark;
like sand blowing in a whirlwind.

My head bound up with horror, I said,
"Teacher, what is it I'm hearing?
Who are these so beaten by pain?"

He said, "This style of misery
is suffered by the sad spirits
whose lives were neither blamed nor praised.

They are mixed with the despicable
angels neither rebellious, nor
faithful to God, who favored themselves.

Heaven expelled them, that it be no
less fine; and hell's horrors won't have them
for glory the convicts would take of them."

I said, "Teacher, what's the hardship
they mourn so extensively?"
He answered, "I'll explain briefly.

These can have no hope of dying;
their lives such confined blind alleys
they envy the fates of all others.

The world will not allow them fame.
Justice and mercy despise them.
We'll not talk of them. Look and pass on."

I was staring, and saw a flag
running in such speedy circle
it seemed unlikely it would pause.

Behind it came a long parade —
I'd never have thought this many
were ever dismembered in death.

When I'd recognized some of them
I saw and knew the ghost of one
whose cowardice made great refusal.

I quickly knew of certainty
this was the faction of trash
too sorry for God or God's enemies.

This rabble, who never truly lived,
was naked, and much encouraged
by the hornets and wasps around,

which furrowed their faces with blood
that flowed with their tears to their feet
where obscene worms harvested it.

Then I looked beyond, saw people
on the bank of a wide river,
so I said, "Teacher, now let me

know who those are, and what practice
makes them seem as anxious to cross
as I see through the murky light."

He said, "These things will be explained
when our journey is interrupted
at the gloomy river Acheron."

I lowered my eyes with shyness,
afraid my words were too forward;
was quiet till we reached the river.

There, coming toward us in a boat,
was a man grizzled with great age,
yelling, "Too bad for you, damned souls!

Don't hope ever to see heaven.
I take you to the other bank,
of eternal shadow, fire, ice.

You people who are still alive,
sort yourselves out from the dead ones."
When he saw I did not get away

he said, "You have to find other
ferry, other passage, not this one.
Find a more bouyant boat somewhere."

My leader said, "Charon, don't quibble.
This is willed up there, where what's willed
makes possible. That's all you need."

This quieted the wooly chops
on the pilot of the gray river:
but flames wheeled around his eyes.

How those naked, exhausted spirits
lost color, and their teeth chattered,
when they heard Charon's rough words.

They cursed against God, their parents,
the human race, place, time, the root
of their conceiving, and their birth.

Then they gathered themselves together
crying hard, on that bank of rascals
that awaits all who do not fear God.

Demon Charon, his eyes live coals,
beckons them, gathers them all up,
smacking the tardy with his oar.

Like autumn leaves lifting themselves off
one after another, till the branch
sees all its riches on the ground,

so Adam's evil progeny
one by one drop down from the bank
at the signal, like summoned pets.

Then they're off on the dark water.
Before they get over there,
a new crowd gathers on this side.

The courteous teacher said, "My son,
those who have died in God's anger
gather here from every country.

They are eager to cross the river.
Divine justice incites them on
so their fear changes to wanting.

No good spirit ever comes this way:
so if Charon is objecting
you'll know what he is talking about."

His talk finished, the dark landscape
shook so hard, that the memory
still floods me with sweat of terror.

This earth in tears gave up a wind
that flashed with vermilion lightnings,
quenched my ability to feel.

I fell like someone gripped in sleep.

IV

4

The deep sleep in my head was cracked
by loud thunder. I was startled
as you are when wakened by force.

My eyes refreshed, I looked around
when I was up, and I stared hard
to understand the place I was.

What's true is I was on the edge
of a hollow, the abyss of pain,
catchment of endless cries' thunder.

It was dark and deep, filled with cloud,
so looking to see the bottom
I couldn't make out anything.

"We go down into the blind world,"
the poet said, pale as ashes;
"I will be leader. You follow me."

I, noting his changed complexion,
said, "How can I come if you're afraid,
who are supposed to calm my fears?"

"What you take for fear is pity
in my expression, for the anguish
people down there suffer," he said.

"We should go. It is a long way down."
He started, made me step into
the first ring that rings the abyss.

As far as we could hear, here were
no cries other than a sighing
that made the extent of air throb.

This was from pain that the huge crowd
(children, women and men), suffered:
a pain not caused by torturing.

My good teacher said, "Don't you ask
what spirits it is you're seeing?
I want you to know at the outset

these did not sin. Though they have merit,
that is not enough without baptism,
entrance to the faith you profess.

Living before Christianity,
they could not worship God properly.
I, my own self, am one of those.

For this failing, and for no crime,
we are lost. Our pain goes this far:
we live, with no hope, in desire."

When I heard this my heart was sad,
knowing people of great value
were suspended in this limbo.

"Tell me, teacher," I began then,
wanting assurance of the faith
that can defeat every error,

"did someone ever leave, by his own
merit, or another's, to be blessed?"
He knew what my question hinted.

"I was newly in this status
when a powerful man arrived
wearing the crown of victory.

He took the ghost of our first parent;
Abel his son; that of Noah;
Moses, lawgiver, obedient;

Abraham, patriarch; David, king;
Israel with father and children,
with Rachel for whom he worked so;

many others: and made them blessed.
You should know, before these spirits
no human spirits had been saved."

We'd not stopped walking while he talked,
but had passed through the thicket,
as I call it, of crowded spirits.

We'd not gone far from where I slept
when I saw fire stand out against
the whole hemisphere of darkness.

We were still some distance away,
not so far I could not make out
the honorable people there.

"Tell me, for you honor all art
and science, who these are, set off
from the others, in such honor?"

He told me, "The renown of them
still sounds up where you are living,
advances them in heaven's favor."

I heard a voice say, "Acknowledge
the greatest of all the poets.
His ghost, who had left, is returned."

Then the voice paused. There was silence.
I saw four great ghosts come toward us.
They appeared neither sad nor happy.

My teacher began talking. "Look,
the one who is holding a sword,
who leads the three as if their lord,

is Homer, the supreme poet;
after him, Horace, satirist;
Ovid third, and the last, Lucan.

They join in my same profession —
poet — as that lone voice called out.
They respect me, and do well to."

So I saw this fine school convened
by the master of perfect song,
who soars like an eagle above them.

When they'd conversed among themselves
they turned toward me with friendly gestures,
and my teacher smiled at this.

Then they did me still greater honor.
They made me one of their group,
a sixth among such wise spirits.

We walked nearer to the firelight
saying things which silence suits here,
as speaking them there was proper.

We came to a hilltop mansion
surrounded by seven high walls,
these encircled by a fine stream.

This we crossed as if it were dry land.
With these wise men I entered through
seven gates, till we reached green lawns.

People were there, their eyes grave and slow,
bearing an air of authority.
They spoke rarely, in soft voices.

We stepped aside to an open
place, luminous, elevated,
so we could look at all of them.

Right there, on the shining grass,
the great spirits were shown to me.
I glory at having seen them:

Electra and many companions,
among them Hector, Aeneas,
Caesar (in arms, with his hawk's eyes);

Camilla, Penthesilea,
elsewhere; the King of Latium
sat with his daughter Lavinia;

the Brutus who drove out Tarquin;
Lucretia, Julia, Cornelia,
Martia; Saladin off by himself.

When I looked up a bit higher
I saw the teacher of thinkers
sat with his philosopher kin.

Everyone looks to him with honor.
Plato and Socrates I saw
stood nearest him, before the rest:

Democritus of the chance world; Thales,
Diogenes, Heraclitus, Zeno,
Empedocles, Anaxagoras;

saw that collector of healing plants
Diascorides; and Orpheus,
Cicero, Linus, Seneca;

geometer Euclid; Ptolemy,
Hippocrates, Galen, Avicenna;
Averroes, great commentator —

I can't describe them thoroughly;
a longer subject pursues me:
my words often less than the fact.

The group of six reduced to two,
my canny guide leads me away
from quiet to the quaking air.

We come to where no light is shining.

5

I climbed down out of the first ring
to a second, enclosing less
space, and pain that provokes wailing.

Minos stands horribly, growling,
weighing the crimes of the entrants,
judging, sentencing with tail twines.

The ill-born spirit before him
confesses all. This conoisseur of sin
sees what place in hell fits the crime

and wraps his tail around himself
as many turns as the degrees down
he directs the sinner to go.

Invariable crowds wait for him.
Each spirit takes its judgment singly:
speaks, listens, and then is cast down.

Minos, when he saw me, left off
this act of his great office; growled,
"You come to a hospice of pain.

Watch how you enter, whom you trust.
Don't let the wide entry fool you."
My guide said, "Why should you object?

Don't block a journey made by fate.
This is willed up there where what's willed
makes possible. That's all you need."

Now the sounds of suffering started
to flood my hearing. I'd come
where loud cries were clashing on me

(all light was snuffed out where I was),
crashing like sea under storm,
the waves and the wind in combat.

This ceaseless nether whirlwind
takes spirits into its current,
tortures them with a brutal flight.

When they attain this violence
there they shriek and complain and cry,
blaspheming the power of God.

I was told those tortured this way
are damned for sins of the flesh
that submit reason to appetite.

It's like crowding flock of starlings
in cold weather, their wings flailing:
that's this wind for evil spirits.

It blows them in random turbulence,
uncomforted, and without hope
either of rest or of less pain.

Cranes creak in flight, and their crying
marks their long passage through the air,
as did the ghosts I saw coming

carried along on the storm.
So I asked, "Teacher, who are these
people so battered in black wind?"

"The first of those you want news of
was empress over the peoples
of many countries, languages.

Such addict of luxury she was,
her laws made license be lawful
to obscure the blame she incurred.

She is Semiramis. We read
she was wife to, and succeeded, Ninus;
held the lands Sultan disciplines.

That other killed herself for love,
broke faith with Sichaeus' ashes.
There is lecherous Cleopatra;

that is Helen, on whose account years
of disaster; great Achilles,
who lastly took on love, and lost.

Then Paris, Tristan..." he showed me
more than a thousand, and named them,
love separated from this life.

But as I heard my instructor
name the ancient knights and ladies,
I was bewildered by sentiment.

I said, "I wish I could converse
with the two who drift together
coupled so lightly on the wind."

"You'll see when they are closer," he said.
"They will come if you call in the name
of the love that is bringing them."

As soon as the wind blew them near
I said, "Wind-driven spirits,
come talk with us if it's allowed."

Doves summoned by their desire
lift firm wings to the downy nest.
Their wills direct them through the air.

They came through wind of the wicked,
so strong the call of affection,
leaving the crowd where Dido was.

"Gracious and kindly animal
come through this black air visiting
us, who have stained the earth with blood;

we'd pray peace for you from the king
of all, if he were friend; for you
pity us in perverse evil.

As long as this wind is slackened
we'll speak with you, and we'll tell you
as much as it pleases you to hear.

The city I was born in lies
at the shore where the Po's waters
and tributaries fall towards peace.

Love takes the kindly heart quickly;
took him in with the sweet body
that is stripped from me, to my shame.

Love allows no lover excuse
from loving; gave me such pleasure
in him, that he can't let me go.

Love led us to a single death.
Caina waits for our murderer."
Their words floated across to us.

When I'd heard these damaged spirits
I looked down and away so long
the poet said, "What are you thinking?"

I began, "Such sweetness in thought,
and so much longing, have brought them
so sorrowful a conclusion!"

And then I turned to them again.
"Francesca, your torturing
makes me cry for sadness, pity.

Tell me, while your sighs were for sweetness,
in what ways did love make you aware
of your unfocused desirings?"

She said, "As your instructor knows
there's no pain greater than recall,
in misery, of happy times.

Since you ask to understand it
I will try to talk through my crying;
tell the origin of our love.

One day we were reading for pleasure
of how love enmeshed Lancelot.
We were alone, suspecting nothing.

Often our eyes met over words
and we blushed. One special passage
it was that overcame us both:

when we read that the longing smile
be kissed by such a lover, he
who'll never be parted from me

kissed all my trembling mouth. The book
and author were our Galahad.
That day we read it no further."

One spirit spoke while the other
cried so, that a deep sympathy
of mortal faintness came on me.

I fell as a dead body falls.

VI

6

When my consciousness returned,
having been drowned in confusion
at the torment of those in-laws,

as I walked I saw new tortures
around me everywhere I looked;
and more spirits being tortured.

I had come to the third ring,
that of eternal rain; heavy,
chill, cursed, and unvaryingly new.

Gross hail, snow, and filthy water
are dumped through the shadowy air;
make a stinking, receptive mud.

Cerberus, a wild beast, fierce and odd,
with three dogs' gullets bays over
the people wallowing in there.

Vermilion-eyed, beard black with filth,
big-bellied, with clawed fingers
he rakes the spirits, flaying their skin.

Rain makes them howl like dogs, and shift
to shield one side with the other:
the rascally trash keeps turning.

This dragon, Cerberus, saw us,
gaped his mouth open, showed his fangs;
began shivering all over.

My guide reached down into the mud,
took handfuls of it, and threw them
into the dragon's starving jaws.

Immediately the foul chops
of the demon Cerberus, so
raucous the damned would be deafened,

quieted — like the dog who barks
from hunger and then falls silent
when it's ravening at its meat.

Stepping on vacant forms that appeared
human, we walked on the spirits
bogged down under this heavy rain.

They sprawled supine, except one spirit
who sat upright when he noticed
we were passing in front of him.

"Recognize me," he said, "If you can,
made before I became unmade,
now guided through this underworld."

It may be your kind of torture
is blurring my recollection.
I feel I've not met you before.

Tell me who you are, put down here
in this sorry place of such pain
worse pain can't be more disgusting."

"Your city," he said, "so crammed full
of envy as to burst its seams,
contained me in easy living.

Your citizens called me 'Piggy.'
Because of my damned gluttony
I am abandoned to this rain.

My sorry soul is not alone.
All these suffer similar pain
for similar sins." He was quiet.

"Piggy," I said, "your suffering
tempts me to tears. If you can, tell
what will become of our Florence,

divided as it is? Is there one
just person there? And what causes
such discord to tear the city?"

"After long tension," he answered,
"They'll come to blood; the woodland party
hound out the other cruelly.

After three years this other faction
will supersede again, by force
of one who tests the weather now.

They'll be in the ascendant
some time, oppress the other party
however they may cry in shame.

There are two just ones, disregarded.
Pride, envy, avarice inflame
all others' hearts in their three fires."

His statement ended in crying.
"Give me some further word," I said.
"There's more that you can teach me

of Farinata, Tegghiaio,
Rusticucci, Arrigo, Mosca;
others who worked to do good things.

I'm truly eager to find out
if heaven comforts or if hell
torments them. Where are their spirits?"

"Theirs are among the darkest souls
whom other sins draw to the abyss,
where, if you sink so far, you'll see them.

When you are in the world's comfort
recall me to my fellows' minds.
I'll say and answer no more now."

Then the directness of his eyes
wavered. He glanced at me, nodded,
fell to blindness with the others.

"He'll not rise again," my guide said,
"till the sound of the last trumpet,
when the angel calls to judgment.

All will find their sad graves again,
put on their flesh and their features
to hear their eternal sentence."

And so we crossed this stinking soup
of ghosts and rain. We walked slowly,
touching upon life after death.

"Teacher," I asked him, "will their torture
increase after the last judgment,
modify, or remain the same?"

"Consider your old formula:
the more perfect the thing, the more
it can feel the good — or the pain.

The damned will be closer to perfect;
though they'll not attain perfection
their pain will be more exquisite."

We followed the circling road
saying more things I don't repeat;
reached the edge of the next downgrade,

found Plutus, arch-enemy, waiting.

VII

7

Plutus started in babbling, "Papey
Satan, aleppey Papey Satan."
My kind instructor understood;

to reassure me, said, "your fright
can't hurt you. Such as his power is,
he'll not stop our descending the crag.

Quiet, damned wolf!" he said, turning
to confront those blustering lips.
"Eat yourself out with your anger.

We do not go down without cause.
It is willed up there where Michael
took vengeance on the result of pride."

Sails bellied out with wind collapse
to rags when the mast cracks, the same
as Plutus now slumped to the ground.

We climbed down to the fourth pocket
that holds more painful content of this
sack of the universe's evil.

Oh, justice of God! What sufferings!
Pain in such bounty for few words!
How our guilts bring us destruction!

Here the ghosts are compelled to reel
a round dance; beat against each other
like the waves over Charybdis.

Here I saw more people than before,
yelling, wheeling great weights around,
pushing against them with their chests.

They crashed against each other, turned,
shouted, "Hoarders!" or "Squanderers!"
and wheeled their weights the other way,

rolling the dark circle to a point
on the opposite side, where they yelled
their shameful rebukes once again.

They turned themselves around at mid-
circle, circled back for the next shock.
I felt that shock against my heart,

said, "Tell me, who are these people?
These on the left who have tonsures,
were all those from the clergy?"

My teacher said, "In their first lives
they were so squint-eyed in mind, they'd not
spend in reasonable amounts.

Their voices yell this out clearly
at the places they meet and turn
where opposing sins confront each other.

Yes, those with tonsures are clergy,
both popes and cardinals, in whom
avarice runs most rampant."

"In that case, I should recognize
some from among this collection
who were made filthy by these crimes."

He said, "Your idea is vain:
dirtied by an unselecting life,
now you can't select amongst them.

They will run both tracks forever.
Some will rise up out of their graves
tight-fisted; and some lacking hair.

Evil in gift or grasp of the world's
bounty has taken it from them,
and leaves them to this buffeting.

Now, son, you see the quick charade
of wealth, which is in fortune's keeping,
and humans struggle after so.

All gold that has been under the moon
would give respite to not even
one of these weary spirits."

"Teacher," I said, "explain the nature
of this fortune you have mentioned,
who keeps control of the world's goods."

He said, "You foolish creatures,
you are so burdened by ignorance —
let me spoonfeed you some wisdom.

The one whose wisdom transcends all
made heaven, and guides its motions
so each of its bodies shines throughout

in uniform distribution.
In the same way for the world's fine things
an administrator is provided

who regularly transfers wealth
from race to race, blood kin to stranger,
despite what schemes humans propose.

One country rules and one weakens
according to that power's judgment,
which is hidden like a snake in grass.

Your mind has no purchase on it.
It supplies, orders, carries out
its control, like any of the gods.

Her transfers, by necessity,
are swift and without a reprieve.
She keeps the shifts of wealth frequent.

It is fortune that's so complained of
even by those who should praise her,
who abuse and blame her bitterly.

Since she is blessed she won't hear them.
Content with those created first,
she turns her wheel in pure delight.

Now come down to worse suffering.
We cannot stay here long. Every star
that rose as I started, is setting."

We crossed the ring. Its other side
banked a boiling spring that emptied
into the trench it cut away.

We, forming company with the dark
water, blacker than persian dye,
accompanied its strange course downward.

It runs into a marsh called Styx,
this sad stream, after it's fallen
to the foot of evil gray cliffs.

I stood trying to see clearly.
Slimy people were in the marsh.
Naked, and with affronted faces,

they beat each other with their fists,
also their feet, heads, chests; they tore
each other to shreds with their teeth.

My teacher said, "Son, now you see
spirits anger has defeated;
and you must also recognize

people under the water sigh
and make the surface of it seethe
as you see when you look around.

Stuck in the mud they say, 'In sweet
air gladdened by sun, we grumbled,
festered with indolent conceit.

So we're depressed now in black slime.'
Except they only gargle this.
Mud prevents them from forming words."

So we walked the filthy reservoir's
great arc, between dry land and swamp,
looking in at the mud-eaters.

Finally we reached a tower's base.

8

We had already seen the top
of the tall tower, I should say,
before we arrived at its foot,

because two flames were burning there,
which another distant beacon
answered, almost out of sight.

I turned to the sea of wisdom,
"What do these signals say? What answer
burns there, and who lit the fires?"

"If marsh mist does not obscure it,
you can already see what comes
across this filthy water," he said.

I saw a little skiff made toward us,
urged on the way a bow's loosed string
thrusts arrow away through the air,

under the guidance of a sole
helmsman, who was snarling aloud,
"Hey, wicked spirit, I've got you!"

"Flegias, Flegias, you're yelling
for nothing this time," my guardian
said. "We're only yours for the crossing."

Flegias swallowed his anger
like those who must incorporate
deceptions, though they resent them.

My guardian stepped into the skiff
and had me board it after him.
Only then did it seem laden.

Once my guide and I were boarded
the old prow cut along, deeper
than with its customary load.

As we crossed the stagnant marsh
someone caked with mud confronted me,
"What premature arrival are you?"

I answered, "I'm passing through.
Who are you, become so filthy?"
"I am The Weeper, as you see."

"Damned spirit, I recognize you,
even covered up with sewage.
Remain the weeper in your grief."

He snatched with both hands at the boat.
My guide fended him off cleverly,
said, "Get down with the other dogs."

Then he embraced me, kissed my face,
and exclaimed, "I know your insult.
She was blessed when she carried you.

That man was arrogant in the world.
No value graces his memory.
So his ghost is here in fury.

Many thinking themselves earth's kings
will lie down like pigs in this swamp
leaving reputations as dirty."

I said, "Teacher, I would be pleased
to see him stuck back in the soup
before we finish this crossing."

"Your wish should be granted," he said.
"You will have that satisfaction
before we touch the farther bank."

Immediately I saw such hash
made of him by the mud people
that God still has my praise and thanks.

"Get that Filippo Argenti,"
they yelled. The wrathful Florentine
even turned on himself with his teeth.

I'll say no more than we left him.
I peered forward, eager to see
what caused a new shout of grieving.

My teacher said, "Now, my son,
we approach the city of Dis
with its crowds and dark citizens."

I said, "Teacher, I see its mosques
there in the valley, vermilion
as if fresh out of the fire."

"The eternal fire burns in them
showing them ruddy to you
this deep down in hell," he told me.

Our skiff had reached the steep earthworks,
defense of this desolate place
whose walls appeared made of iron.

After a long circuit, we came
to where our helmsman yelled loudly,
"Get out. This is where you enter."

Thousands of fallen angels I saw
who shouted in front of the gates
peevishly, "Who, without dying,

comes through the kingdom of dead people?"
My guardian wisely gave a sign
he wished to converse privately.

Their resistance mollified some,
they said, "You come alone. He goes,
who's come here with such arrogance.

He can go back on folly road
alone, or try; since you'll stay here,
who led him through the dark country."

Reader, you may now imagine
how these cursed words alarmed me
to believe I'd never return.

"Oh, my dear guide, you've already
rescued me from contrary risks
and saved me from so many dangers:

don't leave me," I said, "or I'm lost.
If we can't go any further
let's go back quickly together."

The guardian who had led me there
said, "Don't worry. Our right of passage
comes from a source they can't defy.

Wait for me here. Comfort your weary
spirit with the good food of hope.
I'll not leave you in this deep world."

He left, abandoning me there,
my gentle father. Assent struggled
against dismay inside my head.

I could not hear what he told them,
but they rushed inside in disorder
before he'd been with them for long.

The obstructionists slammed their gates
in my guardian's face. He turned back
slowly toward me, hesitating.

He looked down. Now his expression
was not bold as before. He sighed,
"Who locks me out of pain's estate?

Don't be alarmed at my dismay,"
he said. "Whatever obstacle
they offer, I'll overcome it.

This arrogance is their custom.
You've passed one gate they defended
that is now missing its fastenings.

You read the mortal warning there.
Already someone, without guide,
is passing downward through the rings.

He'll open this city to us."

9

My guardian, seeing that I blanched
with timourousness at his set-back,
conquered his own expression.

He was listening carefully,
his eye unable to penetrate
the air's darkness and the thick fog.

"We are obliged to prevail.
If not..." he said... "But no, some help
offers..: though he is slow in coming."

His second phrase masked the intent
of the words he had started with —
a very different message.

So what he said made me anxious.
I found in his broken sentence
perhaps worse meaning than it held.

"Does anyone ever come down
to this level of pain, from the first
whose only pain is loss of hope?"

I posed him this question. He said,
"Rarely does any of us
follow the path I've led you on.

Once before I was conjured here
by that cruel witch Erictho
who called ghosts back to their bodies.

Scarcely was I naked of flesh
when she made me pass through that gate
to take a soul from Judas' ring.

That is the deepest place, the darkest,
farthest from the all-circling sky.
I know the road well, be assured.

The marsh winds its coil of stinking
all around this city of pain.
We can not get in without struggle."

He said more, but my attention
was drawn up to the tall tower
where the beacon was burning.

There, that moment, three furies appeared,
hellishly stained with blood, their limbs
and gestures those of human women,

belted with bright green serpents,
their hair horrible with vipers;
their bestial heads wrapped up in them.

"Those are the Erinyes," he said,
having good cause to recognize
these servants of the queen of tears.

"Megaera is on the left side.
She weeping on the right is Alecto;
Tisiphone is between them."

The furies clawed at their breasts,
beat themselves with their fists and shrieked.
Alarmed, I huddled by the poet.

Glaring down at me, they shouted,
"Medusa come! And make him stone!
Let's take our revenge on Theseus!"

"Turn around. Keep your eyes covered.
If Gorgon appears; if you see her;
you'll not be able to return,"

he said: turned me around himself
and, not trusting my hands, covered
my eyes himself with his own hands.

Those endowed with rational minds
will here recognize the teaching
hidden in veils of subtle verse.

Now, over the disturbed water,
a sound broke, terrifying,
making both of the shores tremble.

It was sound of wind, impatient
against warmer contrary air,
that thrashes straight into the woods

splintering branches, hurling them.
It carries a proud dust before it,
makes beasts and shepherds run for cover.

He uncovered my eyes, and said,
"Look straight over there, where the fog
is heaviest on the ancient scum."

Frogs, when the serpent approaches,
scatter apart into the water
and crouch down against the bottom.

Now thousands of ruined spirits
fled in the same way when, dry shod,
someone approached across the Styx.

He waved the nasty air away
from his face with his left hand, seemed
to suffer no other discomfort.

I turned to my teacher, knowing
this to be heaven's messenger.
My guide motioned me, "Bow and be still."

With absolute disdain, he reached
the gate, opened it with his staff:
for there was nothing opposed him.

"Refuse of heaven! Despised race!"
he said on that ugly threshold,
"What grounds have you for this insolence?

Why seek to resist against will
that will never be thwarted,
rather will make your pain increase?"

Why struggle with fate? Your Cerberus,
if you recall, was flayed from chin
to gullet for doing as much."

He turned back on that filthy route;
said nothing to us, but appeared
a personage beset by business

more urgent than ours. And we passed
through the fortification, safe
in the wake of his holy spell.

We entered without resistance.
I, being eager to inspect
the nature of this fort's contents,

looked all around me everywhere.
A great field was stretching away
filled with suffering and torture.

Sepulchers dotted the landscape
as at the Rhone's mouth, near Arles;
or near Quarnero, at Pola

where the gulf bathes Italy's border;
so the stretch of field is uneven;
except the tombs were harsher here,

for fires were scattered amongst them
and it made them all glow red hot.
No blacksmith could ask hotter iron.

Their covers had been propped open.
Such terrible cries came from them,
of tortured, desolate spirits!

I said, "Teacher, who are these people
who make themselves known by sad cries
out of the chests where they're buried?"

"These are all the great heretics
of every sect, with their followers.
The tombs are very tightly packed.

Alike are buried together,
their graves appropriately heated."
He turned. We walked toward the right,

between the ramparts and the graves.

X

10

I followed my guardian's lead
between earthwork and sepulchers,
single-file on the narrow track.

"Example of holy strength," I said,
"leading through rings of infamy;
please speak to my need for knowledge.

Can we look at those lying here?
All of their lids are propped open,
and no one is keeping guard."

"When they bring their bodies back down
from judgment at Jehosaphat
the tombs will be closed over them.

This part of the graveyard contains
all of his sect, with Epicurus,
who hold the soul dies with the body.

So your questions will be answered:
those you have spoken, and the one
that is still hidden in your heart."

I said, "Dear guide, I'm not hiding
my heart. I'm trying to speak briefly
following your own example."

"Tuscan, you speak honestly, walking
alive in this village of fire.
Please stop a moment if you don't mind.

Your dialect shows you to be
a native of the fine country
I may have harmed too greatly."

The voice issued up suddenly
out of a sepulcher. Startled,
I edged close to my guardian.

"What's the matter?" he said. "Turn around.
It is Farinata rising there,
who'll be visible from the waist up."

My eyes met Farinata's eyes.
He was emerging, head, then trunk,
as if he had no use for hell.

The vivid, quick hands of my guide
thrust me towards him between the crypts.
"Watch how you speak to him," he said.

I stood at the base of his tomb.
He considered me disdainfully,
then asked, "What stock do you come from?"

I was glad to comply, witheld
none of my ancestry from him,
at which he looked at me quizzically.

"They were implacably opposed
to me and my parents, my party.
I routed them on two occasions."

"Both times they reassembled,"
I returned. "Although your people
seem not to have learned this talent."

Beside him a spirit's face
rose, visible only to the chin:
I believe he was on his knees.

He looked around, as if trying,
apparently, to discover
if there was someone else with me.

Disappointed, he cried, "If great
genius earns you this tour of blind
prison, why's my son not with you?"

"It's not on my own I come here.
The one waiting there has brought me.
Perhaps your Guido discounted him."

His words and method of torture
had let me infer who he was,
so that I could answer fully.

He jumped up quickly crying, "What?
You said 'Discounted'? My son's dead?
Sweet light no longer beats his eyes?"

When he saw I hesitated
to answer, he fell supine again,
did not appear any more.

The other spirit, more patient,
at whose instance I had lingered,
did not alter his expression,

took up where we'd been interrupted.
"If my people still lack that skill
it saddens me more than this bed.

You will know to your cost what they can do
before the queen moon, who reigns here,
has become full fifty times more.

And tell me, in case you should reach
sweet earth again, why are their laws
so cruelly against my people?"

"The river Arbia ran blood
from your butchers — therefore exile
for them is preached in our churches."

He shook his head, sighed, "I did not
act alone; nor would I have moved
with the others without reason.

But when the others wished to destroy
Florence, then I, acting alone,
openly defended the city!"

"May your descendants still find peace,"
I said. "But can you untangle
a problem that has perplexed me?

Am I correct that you foresee
what time in the future will bring,
though time present you cannot see?"

"Our vision is impaired. We see
events that are distant. The Lord,
the source of light, allows us this much.

Our minds are blind to things current
or in near time. We need others
to tell us your human affairs.

You can conceive the complete death
that will come to what we can know
when our covers close the future."

Then, regretting my misjudgment,
I said, "Tell the one who fell back
his son is one with the living.

I hesitated to reply
because I was confused about
the subject that you have explained."

My teacher beckoning to me,
I quickly asked the same spirit
to tell me who else lay there with him.

"I lie with more than a thousand:
The Cardinal; Frederick the Second
among them. Of the others, silence."

He withdrew. I moved to rejoin
the old poet, thinking over
the hostile prophecy I'd heard.

He asked me as we went forward,
"What are you so concerned about?"
I answered him quite candidly.

"Keep in mind what you've heard that bodes
you ill," he ordered, wagging his finger.
"And keep it in expectation

of when you achieve the vision
of the woman whose eyes see all.
She will explain your life's journey."

Then he led us off to the left,
leaving the rampart, moving inward
on a track that broached a hollow.

Its squalid reek assaulted us.

XI

11

We walked the edge of a steep cliff,
a ring of giant, broken stones,
and reached a group more tormented.

Because the stink that was rising
from the hollow was overwhelming,
we edged up using the cover

of a tomb on which was inscribed,
"I hold Pope Anastasius,
drawn from the true path by Photinus."

"We might well put off our descent
until our senses are somewhat
inured to the unpleasant smell,"

my teacher said. "Then we should find
some compensation for lost time,"
I said. "I have that well in mind,

my son. Look, this ring of boulders
surrounds three terraces, concentric
like those you have already crossed.

They all are filled with damned spirits.
So that your witness will be informed,
I'll explain how and why they're kept here.

Defiance is the intention
of every evil. Each such intent
does harm, by violence or deceit.

Deceit is evil peculiar
to humans; most despised by God.
The deceitful suffer deeper down.

The first terrace is for the violent,
built in three rings, since violence
has three kinds of personal object:

God, one's self, or one's neighbor —
their persons or their property.
Violence against one's neighbor's

person, is death or injury:
against his property, destruction
by fire, or through extortion.

The first ring segregates murderers,
those who injure people, and thieves,
plunderers; and makes them suffer.

A person does violence against
one's self or goods. In the second
ring, repenting in vain, are those

who deprived themselves of your world:
wastrels and profligates. They weep
who should have been most delighted.

Violence against the deity
is denial or blaspheming;
despising nature and its bounty.

Sealed in the inmost, smallest ring,
are sodomites and usurers
and those who despise God in their hearts.

Deceit undermines conscience,
and may be practiced on the trusting
as well as on the untrusting.

Deceit against the untrusting
breaks the bond of natural love;
so the second terrace harbors

hypocrites, flatterers, witches,
perjurers, simoniacs, pimps,
swindlers, grafters, cheats and such rubbish.

Those who deceive the trusting
reject natural love, and more;
they reject the contract of trust:

in the smallest terrace, pit of Dis,
the low point of the universe,
traitors are consumed forever."

"Teacher, your explanation's clear,
and excellently makes specific
this chasm and the people it holds.

Explain, though, those mired in marsh,
the wind-driven, the rain-battered,
those who crash weights against each other.

If they're in God's anger, then why
aren't they in the burning city?
If they're not, why should they suffer?"

"Is your mind wandering?" he said.
"You are seldom so far off course.
What has bewildered you so much?

Don't you recall the definitions
your *Ethics* uses, concerning
three dispositions heaven forbids:

incontinence; malice; ruthless
bestiality. Least blameworthy
is incontinence: it offends God least.

Think of this logic, and recall
who they are who suffer punishment
up there, outside the city of Dis.

You will understand why they are kept
from these felons, and the divine
vengeance falls less heavy on them."

"You are a sun clearing confused sight
so pleasantly, that my questioning
is grateful as what I know.

Would you develop the idea
from some time ago, that usury
offends divine generosity?"

"Philosophy, if you attend,
consistently demonstrates
that nature takes its direction

from divine wisdom and its works.
You will have noted in your *Physics*,
not many pages from the start,

that artifice of humans, where
possible, follows God's example —
your artifice is God's grandchild.

By these two principles, if you bring
first *Genesis* to mind, it behoves
us to make our living and increase.

The usurer does otherwise,
despising nature and her pupil,
hoping in other principles.

Follow me now, I'd like to go.
The fish glide on the horizon,
the wagon lies to the northeast.

We still have a cliff to climb down."

XII

12

The crag we were meant to descend
was mountain-like. And there lay on it
a shape that would make your eyes quail.

It was like the ruin made by shock
of earthquake, or from slipped support,
when Adige's hillside fell, near Trent.

The rock's been so displaced, broken,
from crest down to the valley floor,
you can find a staircase downward.

Such was our path to the next level:
but stretched out across its beginning,
on broken crag: Crete's infamy,

conceived in the pretended cow.
When he saw us he bit himself,
like one eaten out by anger.

My guardian called to him, "Perhaps
you mistake this man for the Duke
of Athens, who killed you on earth.

Stand aside, Monster! This person
has not come with your sister's guidance,
but goes down to visit your tortures."

The bull, at receipt of the death blow,
breaks loose and plunges in place
but cannot move, in the same way

the Minotaur did now. My guide
saw this, said, "Quick, run! Get onto
the path while he's beside himself."

We found our way down the ruin
of stone. The stones shifted under
the unaccustomed weight of me.

As I went, I wondered. "You may
be speculating on this ruin
watched by the beast's rage I quelled," he said.

"When I came down to deep hell
that other time, you realize,
these rocks had not fallen yet.

Just prior to the arrival
of the one who rescued from Dis
the great treasure of the first ring,

this steep, horrible chasm shuddered
so that I thought the universe
felt love, that can convert the world

to chaos, as some would have it.
That instant, here and throughout,
the ancient rock shifted and slid.

Look into the valley. The blood
river winds there, where those boil
who harm others through violence.

Blind greed, and folly of rage,
urge us on in our short lives
to an eternal suffering."

The ditched wide bed twisted its arc
to embrace the entire plain,
as my guide pointed out to me.

In between its bed and the cliff
centaurs armed with bows and arrows
ran in file, as if hunting on earth.

They all pulled up when they saw us.
Three broke from the herd, selecting
arrows, their bows at the ready.

One called from a distance, "Tell me
from there, or I loose my bowstring:
what torture are you coming down for?"

My teacher told him, "Our answer
will be to Chiron, face to face.
You always were too impulsive."

He touched me, said, "That is Nessus,
who died for Dejanira
and used his own blood for vengeance.

Chiron, Achilles' nurse, looking
down at his chest, is in the middle.
The other's Pholus, filled with rage.

Thousands of them circle the bank
shooting souls that emerge from the blood
farther than their sins allow them."

We'd come closer to the swift beasts.
Chiron took an arrow's notched end
to move his beard clear of his jaws,

and so uncover his huge mouth.
He said to his companions, "Notice
the one in back moves what he touches.

Dead people's feet cannot do that."
My guardian stood at Chiron's chest
where both of his natures were joined.

"He is here, the only live man,"
he said, "whom I lead through the darkness
drawn by necessity, not pleasure.

My new authority has come
from a mouth fresh from singing praise.
Mine is no thief's soul; nor is he.

The same authority that lets
us journey through this wilderness,
asks one of your people to guide us,

show us where a ford's to be found,
and carry the man across it,
since he's no spirit to cross by air."

Chiron's bowed head turned to the right,
said to Nessus, "Go back, guide them.
Divert the troops that may block them."

With this close escort we proceeded
on the edge of vermilion
agitation, where the boiling screamed.

The great centaur told me, of those
up to their eyebrows, "They are tyrants
prodigal in blood and looting.

Here they suffer for merciless acts:
Alexander; savage Dionysius,
Sicily's tormentor for years.

That head of black hair's Azzolino's;
the blond one there is Obizzo
da Este, who's life was snuffed out

in the world, by his own stepson."
I turned. The poet said, "Let Nessus
be principal guide. I'll second."

Some little way on, the centaur
stopped above some people who seethed
in blood up as far as their throats.

He showed one spirit off by itself.
"He, in God's presence, let heart blood
that still is running into Thames."

I saw people whose heads and chests
were above the surface. Many
of them I could recognize.

Little by little the blood
shallowed to foot-cooking level.
This was the place we were to cross.

"As you have seen the seethe shallow
gradually up to this point,"
the centaur said, "You should realize

that from here on it gets deeper
until it comes again to where
the tyrants are kept groaning.

There divine justice punishes
Attila, the scourge of the earth;
Pyrrhus, and Sextus; and it milks

eternal tears, loosened by steam,
out of Rinier da Corneto,
Rinier Pazzo, the highwaymen."

He turned and waded back again.

XIII

13

While Nessus was at his crossing
we addressed ourselves to a woods
through which no pathway was marked out.

Not green, but ash-gray its foliage;
branches contorted, twisted,
bearing no fruit, but venomed thorns.

The wild beasts that so hate plowed land
between Corneto and Cecina,
den in less savage thickets.

Brutish harpies nest here, who drove
the Trojans from the Strophades,
predicting their coming hardships.

Broad-winged, human in neck and head,
feet clawed, and great stomachs feathered,
they wailed in this woods of weird trees.

"Once here, you're in the second ring,"
said my teacher, "as you should know
before you go farther — and will be

as far as the dreadful sands.
Keep your eyes open, and you'll see
things beyond what I can describe."

I heard a great wailing,
but saw no people doing it,
and I stopped, completely baffled.

I think he felt I must believe
the voices came from people hiding
behind the trees because of us.

So my teacher said, "If you break
a sprig off of one of these plants,
you will truncate your mistake also."

Stretching my hand out before me
I tore a twig from a large thorn
and the trunk cried, "You're breaking me!"

Dark blood welled up. It spoke again,
"What are you tearing at me for?
Have you no spirit of pity?

This thicket's been made of people.
Even were we spirits of snakes
your hand might have shown some mercy!"

Like a green log that burns at one end
while the other sizzles, hisses
with the steam that is escaping,

the branch where broken issued both
words and blood together. I dropped
the twig, and stood rooted with fear.

"Had he been able to believe
what he only read in my verses,"
my guardian said to the hurt spirit,

"he'd not have raised his hand against you.
I regret this could be believed
only by my suggesting his act.

Tell him who you were. He can refresh
your reputation in the world,
make amends; for he may return."

"Moved by your kind words," the tree trunk
said, "I cannot keep silence. Since
I must speak at some length, excuse me.

I held both keys to Frederick's heart,
as chancellor: so suavely
I locked and unlocked his counsel,

almost all others were kept out.
I kept such faith to my high office
as to forfeit sleep and energy.

That whore, the common deadly vice
of any Caesar's court — envy —
had her whore's eyes spying always;

incited all minds against me.
They in turn encouraged Frederick
to turn my pleased honor to grief.

My soul, prone to be disdainful,
thinking to escape disdain in death,
made the just do himself injustice.

By these new wooden roots, I swear
I never broke faith with my lord,
who deserved this honor from me.

If either of you should return
to the world, restore my memory,
still prone from envy's mortal wound."

There was a pause. The poet said,
"As long as he is silent, talk,
take advantage, ask what you like."

"I cannot. Pity's too strong.
You continue, asking whatever
you believe will satisfy me."

"So this man will willingly do
the favor you asked," my guide said,
continuing, "imprisoned spirit,

tell how the spirit can be joined
to this gnarled wood; and, if you will,
if any are freed from these limbs."

The tree gave out a deep sigh,
then directed that air to speech.
"My answer to you will be brief.

When the self-violent spirit leaves
its body, uprooting itself,
Minos sends it seven levels down.

It falls in woods, in no select place,
but wherever fortune tosses;
where it sprouts like a seed of rough wheat.

It grows to sapling and wild tree.
The harpies, feeding on its leaves,
make pain, and openings for pain.

Like others, we'll get our bodies;
but not use them again. Justice
won't let us have what we threw away.

We will drag them here. Our bodies
will be hung up throughout the woods
from the thorns of their harmful spirits."

We still listened to the tree trunk,
believing it wished to speak further,
when we were startled by an uproar.

The same way, the hunter in hiding
hears the boar and the chase coming:
beast noise and crashing of branches.

Then two men, naked and scratched, burst
running on the left, so strongly
as to break the branches from the trees.

"To me! Death! To me!" the leader yelled.
The other, following too slow,
called out, "Lano, your legs were not

so quick at the battle of Toppo."
Then, his wind failing him perhaps,
he hunched himself into a thorn.

Behind them, the woods filled up
with black dogs, ravening, running
like greyhounds breaking from their leashes.

They bit at the cowering man,
ripped him apart, chunk by chunk,
carried off the afflicted limbs.

My escort took me by the hand
and led me to the thorn, that wept
uselessly through its bleeding breaks.

"Oh, Giacomo da Sant'Andrea,"
it said, "Why make your shield of me?
Your ugly life's no fault of mine!"

When my guide stood by it, he said,
"You, speaking blood with painful words
out of such wounds: say who you were."

"Spirits, who have come to witness
the shameful destruction of leaves
from my stripped branches: gather them

and heap them at my sorry foot.
I am from your city that changed
its patron Mars for the Baptist,

for which Mars bears a working grudge.
The citizens who rebuilt it
over the ashes Attila left

would have done their work for nothing
did not some image of Mars last
where the Arno river is crossed.

I made a gallows of my house."

XIV

14

Impelled by my benevolence
for our native place, I gathered
the scattered leaves to the worn spirit.

We went on to the boundary
dividing second from third ring;
saw awful instrument of justice.

To demonstrate this new place well
let me say we came to a barren
that forbade bedding to all plants.

The forest of sorrow wreathes it,
is ringed in its turn by the blood stream.
Here, near the border, we held up.

The surface was packed, arid sand,
formed in much the same fashion
as Cato's Libyan desert.

Any who read what was laid out
in front of my eyes, must tremble
at this instance of God's vengeance.

I saw great crowds of naked spirits
weeping in their great misery
constrained under diverse sentences.

Those pacing were most numerous;
those who lay down to torture, least —
though pain made them scream more freely.

In slow fall, over the whole desert,
bulging wads of fire came down
like snow on a windless mountain.

Alexander, in India's
tropics, saw such flames falling
intact onto his troops below.

He had them stamped into the ground
by the men, careful that each flame
be separately extinguished.

Such flames fall here eternally,
setting the sand afire like tinder
under the struck spark; doubling pain.

There was restless dancing of hands
without respite, as spirits slapped
constantly at their fresh burnings.

"Teacher," I said, "you overcome
all but the most powerful devils
who opposed our entrance at the gate...

who is that giant who's lying
in twisted disdain of the fires,
unimproved by such a downpour?"

The giant answered me himself
when he heard me question my guide.
"Dead, I am as I was alive.

Jove will take no joy of his vengeance.
Let him exhaust blacksmith Vulcan
whose lightning he snatched in anger

to strike me with on my last day!
Let him exhaust all the workers
at Mongibello's black forge!

Let him yell, 'Help, help, good Vulcan!'
hurling bolts with all of his strength
as he did at the siege of Thebes!"

"Capaneus," my guardian said,
with a force I'd not heard him use,
"As your pride is unabated,

your punishment is the greater.
Only your own raving frenzy
gives the torture your pride deserves."

He turned back more mildly to me,
saying, "This was one of the seven
kings who besieged Thebes. Then, as now,

he despised God, it would appear.
Let his curses be the medals
he wears for his decoration.

Follow behind me. Be careful
not to step on the blazing sand;
but walk close against the forest."

Silent, we came to a small stream
flowing out of the forest,
whose redness still makes me shudder.

It ran red across the desert
like the brook that the whores share
where it flows from the Bulicame.

Both banks and bed were made of stone
which extended some width beside.
I reckoned this was our pathway.

"Among all the things I have shown you
since we came in through the entrance
whose threshold is refused to no one,

you've seen nothing more remarkable
than the stream I am speaking of
that quenches all flames above it."

After my guide spoke, I asked for
further nourishment, because he
had whetted my appetite.

He said, "A desolate country
lies in mid-ocean, named Crete. Once
the world was pure, under its king.

A mountain is there, once charming
with water and foliage: Ida.
It is deserted ruin now.

Once Rhea chose it as safe cradle
for Jupiter her son. To hide him
she had shouts raised when he would cry.

The Old Man stands in the mountain,
his back turned to Damietta,
staring at Rome as in a mirror.

His head is made of perfect gold;
his arms and chest are pure silver;
then brass down as far as the groin.

From there down he is fine iron,
though his right foot is terra cotta;
standing erect, he favors this one.

But for the gold, each part is split
by a fissure from which drop tears
that, gathering, cut a cavern.

Falling down rocks into this valley
they form Acheron, Phlegethon,
Styx, and then this narrow stream

that flows down till there's no more down,
to form Cocytus. Since you'll see it,
I'll not describe that lake to you."

I asked, "If the stream we see here
has its source up in our world,
why do we first come on it here?"

"You know this place is circular.
The road has been long, but always
leftward and downward," my guide said.

"We've not made a complete circuit.
So if we come upon new things
it should cause you no great surprise."

"Where are Phlegethon and Lethe?"
I asked. "You don't mention the latter;
say the falls becomes the former."

"Your questions please me," he answered.
"This one you might well resolve yourself
by the boiling of the red water.

You will see Lethe, but beyond
the abyss, where spirits can wash
the sins they've repented away.

The time has come to leave the woods,"
he said. "Mind you stay behind me.
The banks make path that does not burn,

and all flame is quenched above them."

XV

15

We walked one of the stone embankments,
a fog from the stream shadowing
embankment and water from flames.

The Flemings, fearing the flood-tide
that threatens between Bruges and Wissant,
have made a similar sea-wall.

The Paduans build such dykes to keep
the swollen Brenta, in the spring,
from flooding their towns and mansions.

These were so structured; not so high
or thick — whoever the architect
might be who had designed them.

We'd come so far from the forest
now, it was out of sight, even
were I to turn and look back.

We came on a crowd of spirits
walking by the embankment. Each
peered at us as, in the evening,

they would by light of a new moon,
squinting like aging tailors
threading the eye of the needle.

While their group examined me
one recognized me, and he caught
my skirt and said, "What a surprise!"

He stretched his arm up in greeting.
I stared hard at his burnt face
so that its scorching not impede

my recognition of the man.
I bent my own face down to his.
"Are you here, Ser Brunetto?" I asked.

"Oh, my son, let Brunetto Latini
accompany you; lag a bit
behind the company he's with."

"With all my heart, if my guide will,
I'll sit down with you, if you'd like.
Indeed, I beg you to do this."

"Any of us who hesitates
an instant, lies under the fires,
can't slap them out, a hundred years.

Keep walking. I'll stay beside you
and then I'll catch up to my group,
weep our eternal ruin with them."

I did not dare climb down to go
on the level he was, but bowed
my head, walked as in reverence.

"What fate or destiny leads you
down here before your final day?
Who is that guiding you?" he said.

"Before my complement of years
in the clarity of open air,
I became lost in a valley.

I left it yesterday morning,
but was heading for it again.
He appeared to lead me home this way."

He said, "If you follow your star,
and if, in life, I saw clearly,
harbor in glory cannot fail you.

If I had not died too soon
I would have encouraged your work,
seeing heaven so kind to you.

The spiteful ingrates formerly
of Fiesole, who retain
its mountain rock in their natures,

will oppose you for your good work;
for the sweet fig should not bear fruit
surrounded by sour-apple trees.

They're known from long back as blind, proud,
avaricious, invidious.
Strip all of their habits out of you.

Destiny prepares you such honor
both factions will be hounding you:
but keep your bait far from the beasts.

Let the Fiesolan cattle
graze on themselves, not the plantings
should they yet grow in their weed patch

where the sacred seed from the Romans
remains, even while the thickets
of their malice are prospering."

"You should still be in human life,
not banished here, Bruno," I said,
"if I could have my wish granted.

Your dear, fatherly example
remains, and distresses me now:
for frequently, while in the world,

you taught me how we make ourselves
eternal. As long as I live
I'll speak my gratitude for you.

I'll write your prediction, keep it
beside the other, for comment
by the woman I expect to meet.

Be assured of my readiness
for fortune, come what may, providing
conscience does not contest it.

This pledge is not new to me. Fortune
may spin her wheel as she pleases,
as the peasant keeps on hoeing."

My teacher turned back, looked at me,
and said, "Whoever takes note
of what he hears, does well to."

Then I continued talking
with Ser Brunetto, asking of
his most notable companions.

"It is good to know some," he answered.
"Others more properly are kept
quiet. Time's too short for great gossip.

These were clerics and notable
scholars of some magnitude,
fouled in the world by the same sin.

Priscian, Francesco d'Accorso
are both in the sorry company.
If you hanker after such scum,

there's bishop of Vicenza, his evil —
strained stem translated from Florence
by the pope, servant of servants.

I would say more, but may not extend
our visit or conversation.
New dust is rising above the sand —

a crowd I must not mingle with.
Please see that my *Tesoro*
is regarded. I live there still."

He turned, like runner at Verona
racing for the green prize ribbon
cross-country: and like a winner,

not like the one who has lost.

XVI

16

The place I'd reached now resounded
with water falling to the next terrace:
a sound like a beehive's hum.

Three of the ghosts running together
separated from their company
under the pain of falling fire.

They came toward us, each one calling.
"Stop! What you're wearing makes you seem
to come from our perverted country."

Such wounds I saw on their bodies,
recent and ancient, burned by flames!
Just the remembering hurts me.

My instructor paused at their speech
and turned to me. "Wait," he said.
"We must be courteous to them.

Did not the place by its nature
shoot fire, I'd expect such impatience
from you, rather than these people."

When we stopped they started moving
their former speed; having reached us,
formed themselves into a circle.

Like athletes stripped naked, oiled,
watching for grip and advantage
before blows and falls are tried,

they circled this way, each keeping
his face toward me, so heads and feet
were in motion constantly.

"If the misery of this place
makes us and our prayers despicable
like our scorched, bald faces," one said,

may our memories persuade you
to tell us who you are, walking
alive safe in this underworld.

The ghost I am walking behind,
naked and flayed as he is now,
was higher in rank than he looks:

He was good Gualdrada's grandson,
Guido Guerra his name. In life
he worked well with sword and judgment.

Treading the desert behind me
is Tegghiaio Aldobrandi
whose advice should have been accepted.

I, placed in punishment with them,
was Jacopo Rusticucci.
My cruel wife drove me to this."

I would have thrown myself down with them
had there been cover from the flames —
I believe with my guide's sufferance.

But fear of the awful burning
overcame my good will, which made me
eager to hug each one of them.

"As soon as my teacher told me
the kind of men who approached us,
your condition transfixed me,

not with contempt, but with such sorrow,"
I said, "it will not be taken
away from me for a long time.

I am from your city. Your acts,
your honored names, I have heard,
and spoken of, with affection.

I pass through bitterness to come
to sweet fruit promised by my guide
after descent to the deep core."

"May your own spirit inhabit
your body a long time; your fame
blaze out behind you," he answered.

"Tell me, do valor and chivalry
live in our city as they once did,
or are they gone forever there?

Guglielmo Borsiere, who joined
our pain recently — he's over there —
has saddened us with his news."

"Florence, your sudden wealth, your new
inhabitants, have generated
excess and pride. Weep for yourself!"

I lifted my face and I cried.
Taking this act for my answer
the three men looked at each other,

and recognized this as the truth.
"Lucky to speak as you will," they said;
"may you speak as freely to others.

If you see open stars again,
returning from this dark country,
and have put all this in the past,

tell people the story of us."
They broke the wheel and ran away,
their legs moving quickly as wings.

Quicker than 'amen' is spoken
they disappeared. My teacher
determined we might move along.

I followed him. In a short time
the sound of close water was so great
we could hardly hear ourselves speak.

The river whose source is Monte
Veso, takes its own eastward route
on the left side of the Appennines,

its upper reach called Aqualietta
before it drops that name at Forli,
and flows into its lower bed,

resounding against the mountain
over San Benedetto, in falls
through a defile where thousands could hide.

Like this, we found, resounding
down its steep cliff, the stained water
loud enough to damage your ears.

I was wearing a belt of rope
I had intended once to use
as a snare to trap the leopard.

After unwinding it from me
as my guide ordered, I coiled it,
made a noose, and gave it to him.

He leaned to his right and threw it
out over the edge of the cliff
into the deep chasm below.

"Some novelty must respond
to this new signal my teacher
follows so carefully with his eyes," I thought.

One should be more cautious with those
who see not only our actions
but can read our inner thoughts.

He said, "You will soon discover
the thing I expect to raise up,
and what your mind speculates on."

A truth that has the look of lie
one keeps private, if possible,
or is blamed, although blameless.

But I can't be silent. Reader,
I swear by this fable's verses
and their hope of lasting favor,

I saw in the dark, heavy air,
astonishing to any firm
heart, a figure swimming upward

as if returning from deep dive
to free the anchor fouled in rock
or other snag on the sea floor,

its arms stretched, and its legs bowed back.

XVII

17

"Look at him: beast with pointed tail,
breaker of weapons, mountains, walls,
and polluting stench of the world."

Saying this to me, my guardian
beckoned him ashore at the end
of the marble causeway we'd walked.

This obscene image of deceit
raised head and chest above the brink
but left his tail hanging below.

His face was that of a just man,
benign on the surface; the rest
of him was reptilian body

with arms furred up to the armpits.
Back, chest, and sides were maculate
in wreaths and labyrinthine knots

gaudier than Turk or Tartar
warp and woof weave into hanging;
or than Arachne's shuttle weave.

Like a beached freight boat, part on land,
part of it still in the water;
or in the same way the beaver

settles down to launch its attack
in the gluttonous Germans' land,
the monster leaned on the sand's stone rim.

His tail frisked into emptiness,
twisted up the venomous fork
that armed its tip like a scorpion's.

"Now our path must bend a little,"
my guide said, "so we can get to
the rascal beast who's resting there."

We took our way down to the right,
keeping ten paces from the edge
to avoid the sand and the flames.

When we came up to the monster
I saw, just beyond him, people
sat next to the open chasm.

"Go and look at their condition,"
my teacher said. "Experience
the ring completely by doing so.

Your conversation should be brief.
Till you return, I'll talk this into
taking us on his strong shoulders."

So by myself I walked outward
to the edge of the seventh ring
where these unhappy people sat.

Tears of pain burst out of their eyes;
their hands ministered, back and forth,
to the flames or the burning sand.

Dogs in summer, bitten by fleas,
gnats, horseflies, worry with muzzles,
hind paws, the way these spirits did.

After looking at several faces
where painful fires were falling,
I knew none of them, but noticed

a purse hanging around each neck,
each with particular design.
They feasted their eyes on these emblems.

Looking as I walked among them
I saw Gianfigliazzi's coat of arms;
a lion azure, on sack d'or.

Also I found Ubriachi's
butter-white goose, on its field
as red as blood, when I looked further.

A spirit whose white purse was stamped
with a sow azure and gravid,
said, "What are you doing in this pit?"

Get out! And since you're alive still
I tell you, Vitaliano
will sit down here at my left side.

I am a Paduan amongst
Florentines who're breaking my ears
shouting, "Come, you most perfect knight

with the three billy goats on your bag!"
He twisted his mouth, stuck his tongue
out, like an ox licking its nose.

Fearing a longer stay would annoy
my guide who'd urged me to be quick,
I turned back from these tired spirits.

I found my guardian mounted
up on the hump of the monster.
He said, "Now you'll have to be brave.

This is our descending staircase!
Climb up in front of me. I'll keep
the middle, so his tail won't hurt you."

Like someone whose malaria
returns, whose nails pale, who trembles
all over at the glimpse of shade:

I was like this. But when he spoke
the shame that makes a servant brave
before a master, gave me strength.

I sat on the monster's shoulders.
"Be sure to hold on," I wanted
to say; but my voice didn't work.

But he, who helped me in other
troubles, as soon as I mounted,
grabbed me and held me with his arms.

"Geryon, take off!" my guardian said.
"Make your descent slow, in wide loops.
Think of the new weight you're carrying."

As boat backs backward from its berth
the monster edged itself off; then,
sensing itself completely cleared,

it turned itself in the air, stretched
its tail out, moved it like an eel
and gathered air in with its arms.

When Phaeton dropped the reins, and let
sky burn — you still see it — his fear
could not have been worse than mine was:

worse than his fear, when Icarus
felt molt of wax melt down his back,
his father yelling, "You're too high!"

Imagine my fear when I saw
nothing but air anywhere;
nothing except for the monster

maneuvering slowly in wheel.
I perceived our descent only
by wind at my face, and from below.

Soon under us, on the right, the gorge
roared terrible crash of water.
I leaned out, twisting my head to look.

My fear of descending increased
at the sight of fires, sounds of cries.
Trembling, I huddled myself down.

Then, as our gyre lowered, beside
narrowing sides filled with tortures,
I began to be able to see.

The falcon who has hovered long
without sighting prey, or the lure —
the falconer calls, "Stoop to me!" —

descends wearily; then quickly
in tighter circles, it comes down
wild and proud, far from its master.

Geryon set us down at the bottom
at the foot of the hacked cliff face
and, unburdened of our bodies,

sprang off like arrow from bowstring.

XVIII

18

The place in hell called Malebolge
is of a ferrous-colored stone
as is the wall surrounding it.

At exact center of this field
gapes a shaft of great width and depth
whose structure I'll tell when we get there.

The shelf I speak of now circles
between shaft and the cliff's foot,
the shelf cut into ten trenches

like earthworks dug in concentric
circles around a fort's walls,
giving an order to the place.

These made a similar pattern.
As such fortresses have bridges
from the gate out to the far bank,

so, from the base of the cliff, causeways
ran, crossing the banks and trenches,
right to the central cutting shaft.

Shaken down from Geryon's back,
this was the place we found ourselves.
The poet headed left. I followed.

On my right I saw new sufferings
filling the first of these trenches:
new anguish, and new torturers.

The naked sinners down there walked two
columns, one toward us, the other
going our way, but moving faster.

(In Jubilee Year the Romans
handled the crowd traffic this way:
one side was for the direction

of the castle and St. Peter's;
and those going toward the mountain
walked the other side of the road.)

Everywhere in the dark rock trench
I saw horned devils with scourges
beat them cruelly from behind.

Didn't the devils stir their stumps
at the first whack! Not one spirit
waited for a second or third.

While I walked my eyes encountered
those of a beaten spirit. "I've seen
my fill of that one already."

Since I had paused to make him out
my guardian waited up for me
and agreed to let me go back.

The beaten one thought he might hide
by nodding, but it didn't work.
I said, "Hey, you, looking at the ground,

unless you're wearing a false face
you're Venedico Caccianemico.
What brings you here to such hot sauce?"

He said, "I speak against my will,
but your straight talk makes me do it.
It brings the old world back to me. 110

It was I who led Ghisola
to do what the Marquis wanted,
however they tell the dirty tale.

Nor am I the only crying
Bolognese here; we're full of them —
more than are tongues that "yes" with "sipa"

between Savena and Reno.
If you want firm proof of this, think
of the avarice in our hearts."

While he spoke, a devil beat him
with his scourge, and said, "Get on, pimp!
There's no women here you can sell!"

I rejoined my waiting escort,
and in a few paces we reached
a spur issuing from our path.

We took this easily enough,
turned right and walked its rocky ridge,
so left the eternal circling.

When we reached the place where there
yawned passage beneath for the beaten,
my guide said, "Wait, and examine

the faces of the other ghosts
you couldn't examine before
since we walked in their direction."

From our causeway bridge we watched them
come from the direction we'd come,
driven with whips like the others.

My teacher, without my asking,
said, "Look at that big one coming.
Pain squeezes no tears out of him.

How much he still looks like a king!
He's Jason, who, with scheming courage
stole the golden fleece from Colchis.

He passed through the isle of Lemnos
after the ruthless women there
had killed all of their males.

There he deceived Hypsipile
with his ornate words and gestures.
(Her deceit had saved her husband.)

He left her there, pregnant, alone.
That sin condemns him to this torture,
which also gives Medea vengeance.

With him are others who practiced
similar deceits. Enough, now,
of this trench and those it's eaten."

Already our narrow pathway
met the top of the second bank
which gave support for the next span.

We heard people moaning, their muzzles
snorting, down inside the next trench,
as they slapped at themselves with their hands.

The banks were crusted with a mold:
caked exhalations from below,
an assault on our eyes and noses.

The bottom was too deep to see
until we had reached the apex
where our rock bridge arched its highest.

From there we could see in the trench
people immersed in excrement
like what runs out of human privies.

When I looked down into it hard
I saw one head so caked with crap
you couldn't tell if it was tonsured.

He yelled, "Why stare more hungrily
at me than the other uglies?"
"Because, if memory serves me,

I've seen you before with dry hair,
as Alessio Interminei
from Lucca — that's why I'm staring."

Then, whacking at his nut, he said,
"Flattery, which never plastered
my tongue enough, drenches me here."

Then my guide said, "Lean out further
so you can fully examine
the features of that woman,

the debauched camp-follower
scratching herself with filthy nails,
who stoops, stands, and crouches again.

It's Thais the whore, who answered
her lover's 'Are you grateful much?'
'Oh, yes! Stupendously grateful!'

Let's say our eyes are satisfied."

XIX

19

Simon Magus! Your despicable
followers prostitute God's things
to gold and money. God's things should

marry with generosity.
Last trumpet, sound for simonists,
and blast them here to the third trench!

We'd already reached the next arch
of the rock bridge, and were standing
above the middle of the trench.

Supreme wisdom, such is your art
shown in heaven, earth, our evil world!
What justice your power distributes!

I saw that the ash-colored rock
was pierced up the sides, and below,
with borings all the same width round.

These were of about the same size
as the chambers at the baptistry
of my lovely San Giovanni,

one of which, not many years back,
I broke to save a strangling child.
Let this word be my guarantee.

From the mouth of each boring stuck
a sinner's feet and legs up to
the calves. The rest was down inside.

The soles of their feet were flaming
making their joints jerk so hard
as to break apart ropes or chains.

From heel to toes flame was moving
as it does on the outer skin
of something covered with oil.

"Teacher, who's that in such torment
he's twisting more than his fellows,
licked by the reddest flames," I asked.

He said, "If you wish, I will take you
down there, by where the bank's less steep.
You can learn his sin and self from him."

"Whatever pleases you is fine.
You be master. Know I won't swerve
from your will. You even know my heart."

When we reached the fourth embankment
we turned and went down on the left
to the joint of the riddled sides.

My teacher kept me beside him
until we had reached the boring
of the fellow who cried with his shins.

"Whoever you are who's keeping
his top parts underneath, planted
like a pole: talk if you can," I said.

I stood like the monk confessing
assassin, stuck head down in his hole,
who calls him back to put death off.

"Is that you already, up there?
That you up there, Boniface?" he said.
"The prophecy's several years off!

You're sated so fast with property
you took the lady church by trick for
before you trashed and wasted her?"

I stood not knowing how to answer,
as people do when they are mocked
but fail to understand what's said.

Then Virgil said, "Quickly, tell him
'I'm not him; not who you think I am.'"
And I responded as he said.

The ghost wrenched his feet completely
and said, in a complaining sigh,
"Then what are you asking me for?

If you are so anxious to know
who I am you climbed down the bank,
know I was dressed in the pope's robe.

True son of the Orsini bear,
I so worked to advance the cubs
in wealth, I've pocketed myself.

Under my head are stuck others
whose simony preceded mine,
crammed into this fissure of stone.

In my turn I'll go farther down
when the pope that I thought was you
when I questioned you, shall arrive.

I've been here upside down, my feet
burning, a longer time than he
will be planted with his feet red.

After him from the west will come
lawless shepherd of ugly works
fit to be plug for both of us.

He'll be like the Jason you read of
in *Maccabees,* his king favored
like this one by the King of France."

I don't know whether the degree
of openness in my answer
was excessive: "Well, how much cash

did our Lord want from St. Peter
before putting the keys in his care?
Surely he asked only, 'Follow me.'

Neither Peter nor the others
asked money of Matthew when choosing
him to the traitor's vacant place.

So stay here. You are well punished.
Carefully guard the bribe money
that stiffened your back against Charles.

If reverence for the great keys
you held while your life was pleasant
did not prevent me from it,

the words I use would be harsher.
For your avarice harms the world:
trampling good; raising up the depraved.

Shepherds like you the Evangelist
John saw, as: She Throned on High above
the Waters, and fucking for kings;

she who was born with seven heads,
having the ten horns' rule so long
as her rectitude pleased her spouse.

You've made god from gold and money.
Where's the idolater different, but
he worships one to your hundreds?

Constantine! What evil you spawned —
not your conversion — but the grant
the first rich pope accepted from you!"

While I chanted him this plainsong,
whether anger or conscience bit him,
he kicked away hard with both feet.

I truly think it pleased my guide
for he listened with a content grin
to the true words as I said them.

He took me into both his arms.
After he lifted me to him
he climbed the path we had come down.

He did not tire of carrying me,
took me up to the next span, crossing
from the fourth to the fifth embankment.

There he put down his burden gently:
gentle on steep and ragged rock
that would make hard going for goats.

From here we could see the next trench.

XX

20

I write lines of new penalties,
subject for the twentieth canto
of my first song — about those below.

Now I was so situated
I could look into the next trench
which was flooded with anguished tears.

I saw in the circular trough
silent and weeping people come
at the world's liturgical pace.

When I looked more carefully at them
they seemed to be strangely distorted
at the joining of chin and chest.

Their faces twisted to their backs,
they were obliged to walk backward,
being unable to look ahead.

Maybe the rigors of palsy
have caused such distortion to some;
but I've not seen, and don't believe it.

If God allows you, my reader,
to take profit from your reading,
imagine! How could I help crying,

seeing our images so near
and so twisted. Their eyes' weeping
bathed the cracks of their buttocks.

Of course I cried, and leaned on a rock
of that hard slope, so my escort
said, "Are you foolish as they are?

Your live sentiment should be dead!
Who is more wicked than the person
who'd twist God's reckoning to his own?

Lift up your head! Lift it up! Look!
Earth opened for that one before,
the Thebans all screaming, 'Amphiaraus,

are you falling away from the war?'
and his fall did not stop till he met
Minos, who snatches each of them.

Look how his shoulder blades serve for chest!
Since he wished to see too far ahead,
he looks behind and walks backward.

Look at Tiresias; changer
of appearance from male to female,
he shifted his members entirely.

He had to strike his staff against
the coiled couple of serpents
before he got his male skin back.

There Aruns backs along against
his stomach. He lived in a cave
of white marble in the mountains

of Luni, where the Carrarese
who live below, farm. Here he could see
the stars and sea without hindrance.

The woman covering her breasts
which you can't see, under ragged hair,
has her hairy parts back there too.

She was Manto. She searched many lands
before settling where I was born;
so I want you to listen a bit.

After her father passed from life
and Bacchus' city was enslaved,
she wandered the world a long time.

High in lovely Italy, at foot
of Alps that close off Germany
above Tyrol, lies lake Benaco.

More than a thousand springs, I believe,
from water standing in that lake,
bathe Garda, Val Camonica, Pennino.

At center is a site where bishops
from Brescia, Verona, Trentino
may celebrate, when they pass there.

Peschiera, a strong, handsome fort
to face the Brescians and Bergamese,
sits where the lake's bank is lowest.

At this point all the water falls
Benaco's lap can't hold, making
river out through green pastureland.

Soon as the water runs from this source
it is called Mincio, not Benaco,
till at Governo it joins the Po.

It runs not far before a lowland
where it spreads out into a marsh,
often miserable in summer.

Manto, raw virgin, passing through,
saw land in the midst of the swamp,
unfarmed and uninhabited.

There, to escape human contact,
she settled with her slaves, practiced
her art, lived, left her vacant body.

Her people, who had been scattered,
gathered to this spot, which was strong
from the swamp that surrounded it.

They made a city on her dead bones;
called it Mantua after her,
considered no other patron.

Once its people were numerous
before Casalodi's foolishness
made place for Pinamonte's tricks.

Should you hear of other versions
of my land's origin, defend
this truth — I assign you this task."

"Teacher," I said, "your recounting
is so sure, and so convincing,
other tales would be dead letters.

Tell me, though, of the people passing,
if you see any worth noting;
my attention is more on them."

He told me, "That fellow whose beard
reaches from cheek to brown shoulders
was an augur in Greece at the time

there were so few males, hardly any
were left in cradle. He, with Calchas, gave,
at Aulis, sign to embark for war: 124

Eurypylus. My tragedy
sings of him in a place you know
since you know the whole song so well.

The other, so narrow-waisted,
was Michael Scot, who truly knew
the fraudulent game of magic.

There's Guido Bonatti; there Asdente
who should have stuck to his shoe leather
and is now regretting too late.

Those are unhappy women who dropped
needle and shuttle, or spindle,
to work charms with herbs and voodoo dolls.

But come! Cain-in-the-moon's thornbush
brushes the water under Spain
at the pillars of the world's end.

Last night the moon was already full,
you should recall; for it assisted
you, now and again, in the deep woods."

So he said as we proceeded.

XXI

21

We went, conversing of other things
my comedy cares not to say,
from one bridge to the next; reached its peak,

stopped to look into the next trench
of Malebolge: the next vain cryings:
found it was amazingly dark.

In the Venetians' arsenal
in winter, viscous pitch is boiled
to daub the seams of leaky ships.

Since the ships cannot navigate
workers replace wood, caulk the hulls
of ships worn out with voyaging.

There's hammering from stem to stern.
Some workers make oars, coil new rope,
mend reef points, and patch the mainsail.

Not heated by fire, but divine skill,
thick melted pitch boiled down there,
and it tarred up the entire bank.

I saw pitch, but nothing in it
but bubbles raised by the boiling
that were swelling up and collapsing.

While I was staring into it,
my guide, saying, "Watch out! Watch out!"
snatched me to him from where I stood.

I turned like a person who hangs back
to watch what he must escape from,
who is weakened by sudden fear,

and won't delay his flight to stare.
Back of us I saw a black devil
running at us on the trench's bank.

What a fierce face he had on him!
His movements so vicious! His wings
spread open, and he paced lightly.

Loaded across his sharp shoulder
he humped a sinner, and clutched him
by the tendons of both ankles.

"To the bridge, Malebranchers!" he called,
"Here's City Councilman of Lucca!
Poke him under while I get more!

I have plenty more of them up there,
all on the take — except Bonturo.
There a 'no' vote turns 'yes' for cash."

He dropped him off the bridge and turned
back on the cliff road, fast as loosed
bloodhound who's hunting the thief down.

The dropped one plunged, bobbed back, twisted.
Devils under the bridge's arch yelled,
"Prayers to the holy face won't help you!

You're not swimming your Serchio here!
If you don't want to taste our points
don't come up above the pitch!"

They stuck him with their hundred forks
saying, "Do your dance under cover.
Rake off your take there if you can!"

In the same way cooks make their helpers
fork the meat chunks down in the broth
to prevent it from floating on top.

My teacher said, "You'd better crouch down,
give yourself screen of this outcrop
so the devils won't see you're here.

If they attack me, don't be afraid.
I understand what happens here,
since I've grappled with it before."

He walked across to the bridgehead,
crossed onto the sixth embankment,
which required a confident approach.

With the bluster and commotion
of dog pack rushing a hobo
who begs fast while he hesitates,

they flocked out from under the bridge
and turned their pitchforks against him.
But he said, "Don't any one dare!

Before you touch me with your barbs
one of you come listen to me.
Then you can think about forking."

All the devils yelled, "Go on, Badass!"
While they stood tight, Badass came out
saying, "What good will this do him?"

"Badass, do you think you'd find me
coming here," my teacher said, "without
security from your pitchforks,

that's clearly provided by God's will?
let me go on. Heaven wills I guide
someone else down this wilderness path."

The devil lost such face he dropped
his fork, and said to the others,
"I guess we can't fork him in, then."

My guide called, "Now, you, squatting
back of the bridge abutment:
you can come safely out to me."

I came out, running to him fast,
and the devils pressed forward so
I feared they would not keep their truce.

I once saw a whole infantry
under safe conduct from Caprona
march trembling so between their enemies.

I huddled my body completely
against my guide's, not taking my eyes
from their unreassuring faces.

They pointed their prongs at me, shrieked
to each other, "Right in the fanny?"
answered, "Sure, give him a good dent!"

The devil who'd been parleying
with my guide, turned to him suddenly,
shouted, "Stuff it! Stuff it, Spitwell!"

then told us, "You can't go further
by this causeway, because the bridge
has crumbled into the abyss.

If you want to go in further
follow the top of this embankment
and you'll find a spur to cross by.

Five hours from now yesterday
twelve hundred sixty-six years back
it was, the next bridge was broken.

I'll make ten of my guys go that way
to see who's out airing themselves.
Go with them. They won't let you down.

Wingdrag and Hoarfoot, step forward,"
he called them, "Step forward, Cur!
Bristlebeard, you lead ten of them!

Lustberry, hup! and Dredgelazy,
Tusker Pokecherry, and Bitchscratch,
Throttlefly and Crazy Rusty!

Go out and search the boiling pitch.
Let these go safe to the next bridge
that crosses the trenches in one piece."

"Oh, teacher, what are we in for?"
I said, "Please, let's go without escort
if you know how. I can do without this!

If you're as sharp as you have been,
don't you see how they grind their teeth
and threaten us with their eyebrows?"

He said, "You need not be frightened.
Let them grind their teeth if they wish.
It's for the boiling sufferers."

They turned left on the embankment
but first each one stuck its tongue out
through its teeth as, "Ready, Captain,"

who, with his asshole, bugled, "Charge!"

XXII

22

I have seen knights shifting camp,
mustering, commencing the assault;
sometimes retiring back in flight.

People of Aretino, I've seen
war horses on your land, marching
foragers, tournaments, and jousts

signaled with trumpets sometimes, bells,
drums, signals from the tops of towers,
native and foreign instruments:

I never saw horse- or foot-soldiers
moved by such dubious bagpipe —
ship follow such landmark or star!

We went with the ten devil's wild
gang — but in church it's with the saints;
in the bar it's with the boozers.

Now I was studying the pitch
to see the contents of that trench
and the people cooking in it.

Like dolphins signaling sailors
with the arching play of their backs:
take care, prepare the ship for storm:

a sinner now and then, to ease
the pain, would show his back, and dive
quicker than a flash of lightning.

And as at the edge of ditch water
frogs rest with just their noses out
so as to hide their bulk and legs,

the sinners crouched in the same way.
When Bristlebeard drew near to them
they slipped back under the boiling.

My heart still shivers at the sight
of one who waited, like one frog
staying while the others make their dash.

Bitchscratch, the closest one to him,
hooked him out by the tarred hair,
held him up like a speared otter.

(I knew them all by name already,
having listened as they were mustered,
and heard what they called each other.)

"Hey, Rusty, put your hooks in him!
Skin him, Rusty!" the devils yelled,
all the cursed crowd in a chorus.

"Teacher," I said, "can you tell me
the name of the unlucky one
who's come to his enemies' hands?" 134

My guardian approached near to him
asking where he was from. He answered,
"Born in the kingdom of Navarre,

my mother, since she conceived me
to a useless wastrel of self
and substance, put me in service

to a lord. Then I was domestic
to King Thibault, and commenced graft
which I account for in this heat."

Tusker, whose mouth issued from each side
tusks like a boar's, let him enjoy
the ripping tear of one of them.

The mouse had fallen to bad cats.
Now Bristlebeard embraced his man
saying, "Stand back while I hold him!"

and turned to my teacher: "Ask him
what more you want to know from him,
before these others rip him to shreds."

My guide said, "Tell me, do you know
if there's a Latian under the pitch
with the other guilty?" He said,

"I just now left one from those parts.
If I still had him for cover
I'd not feel their forks and their claws."

Lustberry said, "Enough of this
patience!" and forked the spirit's arm,
tore out and carried off a muscle.

Dredgelazy tried to take a holt
on the lower leg; their lieutenant
circled around, glaring them off.

When they had been a bit subdued
my guide, without demur, asked him
(he was still gaping at his wound),

"Who was it you had the bad luck
to leave behind when you surfaced?"
He answered, "Brother Gomita

from Gallura, pot for all frauds.
When he had his patron's enemies
in hand, he gave them cause to gloat:

took money from them for himself
and sent them off as smooth as spit:
a grand, not a petty, grafter.

With him is Michel Zanche
of Logodoro. Their two tongues
don't tire of talking Sardinia.

Help! Look at that devil grinning!
I'd talk more, but I'm scared he's set
on raking my mangy hide!"

Their high priest turned on Throttlefly
whose eyes were rolling for the strike;
said, "Keep off, you ugly bird-brain!"

The terrified captive resumed,
"I can make Lombard or Tuscan come
if you want to hear or see them;

but keep them and their pitchforks back
so they can't start punishing me.
I'll stay in this spot all alone

and make seven come by whistling
as our usual practice is
when we get out and see it's safe."

At this word Cur lifted his muzzle,
shaking his head, said, "It's a trick!
He thinks he can escape back in!"

He, with his hoard of trickery,
answered, "What do you mean it's a trick?
Aren't I making my own friends suffer?"

Wingdrag could not contain himself;
said, over others' objection,
"If you dive, I'll not just run after,

but swoop out over the pitch. See
if you alone can outsmart us!
Jump down then! Hide under the bank!"

Reader, here's a new game for you!
All of them glanced away, Wingdrag
first, who had been least prepared to.

The Navarese took this moment,
pushed off from the ground with his feet,
leaped free from Bristlebeard's clutches.

Now the devils saw their mistake,
especially Wingdrag, who caused it,
who started out, yelling, "I've got you!"

without effect: wings won't outdistance
terror. The sinner went under.
Wingdrag looped up his chest in flight.

The duck dives under the same way
at the stoop of the falcon
who rises disappointed, angry.

Hoarfoot, enraged by the farce,
kept flying after Wingdrag, hoping
an escape would cause a scramble.

When the grafter had disappeared
Hoarfoot turned his hooks on his partner
and they tangled above the trench.

But his partner Wingdrag, true raptor,
had claws of his own to sink in,
and the two plunged into the pitch.

The heat of it soon broke their clinch
but they couldn't lift themselves out
for their wings had become so stuck.

Bristlebeard, yelling with the rest,
had four fly across with their forks
and the four, immediately

swooped over the pair on both sides,
poking their forks at the devils
stuck in the crust of scalding pitch.

And we left them in this tangle.

23

Silent, and without our escort,
we journeyed on in single file
like Franciscans on the road.

I was reminded by this brawl
of Aesop's fable, where he tells
of the frog who ferries the mouse.

If one compares the start and finish
of each tale, they're obviously
parallel as "yep" and "yeah" are.

And as one thought leads to another,
still another idea occurred
doubling my original fear.

This was my thought: they've been made fools
on our account — so tricked and hurt
they must be awfully angry.

Add anger on to their ill will
and they'll come after us meaner
than dogs snapping after a rabbit.

I felt my hair on end with fear
already; stood looking back hard,
and said, "Teacher, if you don't hide

me and yourself quickly, I fear
the Malebranchers. They're behind us
so close I imagine I hear them."

"If I were a mirror, your image
could not cross so quickly into me
as I receive your inner thoughts.

Your thinking, entering into mine,
joins with my acts and expressions
so that I make a plan from both.

If the right bank slopes gradually,
we can get down to the next trench.
We'll escape your imagined pursuit."

He'd not finished telling his plan
when I saw them coming with spread wings
not far away, eager to catch us.

My guide immediately caught me up
like a mother wakened by the roar
who sees flames burning beside her.

She grabs up her little child and runs,
caring more for it than herself.
She'll not wait to put on a wrapper.

He slid on his back down the ridge
by rocks that had broken and fallen
like a dam into the next trench.

Not even water runs as fast
when it rushes out through the sluice
over the mill wheel's paddles,

as my teacher went down that rockfall
holding me up against his chest
like his son, not his companion.

He'd hardly set foot on the bed
of the trench when they reached the ridge
above us. But we need not fear,

for that providence placing them
as guardians over the fifth trench
forbids them the power to leave it.

We found colorful people down there
walking the circle very slowly,
crying in a weary defeat.

They were wearing capes with deep cowls
that covered their eyes, in the style
designed for the monks in Cluny.

The cloaks shimmered outside with gold;
but their insides were lead, so heavy
the ones Frederick made would seem straw.

Eternally heavy cloaks! Now
we turned left again, walking with them,
listening to their sorry complaining.

But the people came so slowly
wearied by the weight they were wearing,
at each step we had new partners.

I said to my guide, "Why not find
someone I'd know by name or action?
You can look around as we walk."

One who understood my Tuscan
dialect, called from behind, "Wait,
you're running too fast in this darkness!

You might get what you want from me!"
My guide stopped and turned, saying, "Wait,
and then move forward at his pace."

I stopped. Two of them looked anxious
to join up with us, though their loads
and the narrow path slowed them down.

Having reached us they looked at me,
their eyes aslant, without speaking;
then they turned to each other, saying,

"This one seems living, by his throat's
movement. If he's dead, by what right
is he not weighted by the cape?"

Then they said, "Tuscan, you have come
to the college of hypocrites.
Don't scorn telling us who you are."

I told them, "Born and raised on sweet
Arno, in a great town, I'm here
with the body I've always had.

Who are you, though? I see on your cheeks
such distillation of sorrow;
what is the bright punishment you wear?"

One answered, "Our golden mantles
are lead of such a heavy weight
they'd cause a scale to creak with it.

Brothers of Joy we were, from Bologna.
I'm Catalano; he, Loderingo,
chosen jointly to a post in your town

144

(though a single man is usual),
to maintain the peace. The way we did
is still talked of around Gardingo."

I began, "Brothers, your evil..."
but stopped, for I saw a man
crucified with three stakes to the ground.

He saw me and started to writhe,
blowing exclamations through his beard.
Brother Catalano noticed him,

said, "The nailed man counseled the Pharisees:
'it is expedient one man
should suffer in the people's place!'

He's splayed naked across the road
as you see; his occupation
is to feel our weight as we pass.

His father-in-law is tortured
the same way in this trench, like others
of the evil Council of the Jews."

Then I saw Virgil staring down
at the man stretched out in a cross
in ignominious exile.

Then he said to the monk, "Tell us
if you don't mind, if there is a way
we can get up the next embankment.

We want to leave without obliging
black angels to come and carry us
out of the bottom of this trench."

He answered, "There is a rock bridge
issuing from the great pit, crossing
the wild trenches. It's quite near by.

Being broken, it can't bridge this;
but you can here climb up its ruin
piled from the bottom up that side."

My guide stood looking down a bit.
"Back there, the ones who fork sinners
gave us false directions," he said.

The monk said, "In Bologna I heard
the devil has flaws, among which:
he fibs, being father of lies."

My guide set off with long paces,
looking to be quite moved by anger.
I took my leave of the loaded,

followed the tracks of his dear feet.

XX IV

24

In the year's youthful spring, when sun
warms its rays under Aquarius,
nights shorten towards half the day's span;

frost on the ground makes a mimic
of the forms of her sister, snow.
(Though the frost cannot last as long.)

The peasant, his fodder exhausted,
gets up, looks out over the field,
sees it's all whiteness, slaps his thigh,

returns to his house and groans around —
(The poor thing doesn't know what to do);
steps out again, and hope returns:

he sees the whole world's face is changed
in a few minutes. He takes his stick
and shoos the lambs out to pasture.

My teacher worried me this way
when I saw his face so troubled;
but his anger burned off quickly.

For when we reached the bridge's ruins
his face wore the calm expression
I'd first seen at the mountain's foot.

He chose his route after looking
carefully at the broken rocks.
Then he took hold of me with his arms,

like a careful planner, and one
who makes provision in advance:
for, raising me up to the top

of a boulder, he looked to the next,
saying, "Now you can try that one,
but make sure it will support you."

This was no route for the cloaked ones:
he had no weight; I, with his help,
barely got from one hold to the next.

I don't know about him, but I'd
have been defeated, had not the climb
been shorter than the way down was.

But since all Malebolge is inclined
toward the mouth of that deepest pit,
the nature of each trench is such

the outer wall's higher than the innner.
But we finally reached the point
the last stone had been broken from.

My lungs were so exhausted of breath
when I got up, I could do no more.
As soon as I could, I sat down. 150

"You must forswear sloth," said my teacher.
"Fame does not come to those sitting
on pillows, or under their quilts.

And without fame, life is consumed,
leaves no more print of itself on earth
than smoke prints air; or foam, water.

Get up! Conquer shortness of breath
with a soul that will overcome
if the body does not drag it down.

A longer grade must still be climbed.
It's not enough to leave those people.
Understand. Profit in your action."

I got up, showing second wind
greater than what I felt, and said,
"Go on. I am strong and fearless."

We took the path up the causeway,
narrow, rocky, and intricate;
steeper than the former one was.

So as not to seem feeble, I talked
while walking. Out of the next trench
a voice came, not speaking clearly.

Though I'd reached the next crossing span,
I couldn't make out what it said,
but the speaker seemed to be angry.

I looked down, but my eyes, alive,
could not reach through dark to that depth.
I said, "Teacher, why not lead on

to the next bank, and climb down its face.
I hear something I can't understand;
look down, and can't see anything."

"I will answer by action," he said,
"since a fair request should be followed
silently by its performance."

We got off the bridge at the head
where it abutted the eighth bank,
and there the trench appeared to me.

I saw there terrible clusters
of serpents, and of such strange kinds!
My blood is chilled by the memory.

Lybia's desert has nothing
for all the vipers it may breed —
two-headed; jaculi; pareae —

add the snakes of Ethiopia
and all the land to the Red Sea,
you'd have no such pestilent swarm.

In this cruel largesse, naked
people ran in fear, without hope
of hide, or heliotrope for snakebite.

They were manacled behind with snakes
who thrust head and tails through their loins
and knotted themselves up in front.

Suddenly a person beside us
was struck by a serpent, who bit
the joint of his neck and shoulders.

Quicker than I cross t, dot i,
he kindled, burned, and, falling down,
was completely changed to ashes.

While he lay on the ground destroyed
his dust collected by itself
and quickly took its former shape.

In the same way, wise men agree,
the Phoenix dies, is born again,
when it reaches its five hundredth year.

In life it eats no leaves or other
forage but incense and balsam,
its last nest faggots of nard and myrrh.

Like someone who falls, not knowing
whether a demon's force throws him
or he's tripped on some obstruction:

when he rises he starts staring,
bewildered by the great anguish
he's suffered; gapes around panting:

the sinner stood up in this way.
How severe the power of God
that rains such blows in its vengeance!

My guide asked the spirit who he was,
and he said, "I dropped from Tuscany
to this wild gorge not long ago.

Bestial, not human life pleased me,
mule that I was. Vanni Fucci
the beast; Pistoia my home den."

I said, "Tell him not to sneak off,
guide; ask what crime stuck him down here.
I knew him: angry, bloody man."

The sinner heard me, did not pretend
otherwise, but turned and faced me
with an expression of sad shame.

Then he said, "I am sorrier
you catch me in this misery
than I was to be snatched from life.

I can't refuse what you're asking.
I'm put down so low since I was
thief of the sacristy's furnishings

and others were falsely blamed.
So you'll take no joy of this sight
if you ever escape the dark,

listen to what I'm telling you:
first, Pistoia is wasted of Blacks,
then Florence renews men and means.

Mars brings mist of fire from Val
di Magra, which is wrapped in clouds
and in sudden, bitter tempests.

Battle will be joined on the field
of Piceno, such as to break the mist
and bring harm to every White.

I have said this to give you pain."

25

After he spoke, the robber gave
the finger with each raised fist, yelled,
"Up yours, God! I'm aiming at you!"

From then on the snakes seemed my friends.
One of them coiled around his neck,
a way of saying, "Stop talking!"

Another snake twisted his arms
together again, knotted so tight
the spirit could not jolt them loose.

Pistoia! why not consign yourself
to flames, to exist no longer.
You're worse than those who founded you.

In all of hell's dark rings, I saw
no soul more arrogant to God,
including the giant of Thebes.

He spoke no more, but ran away.
I saw a furious centaur run
shouting, "Where's Hercules?"

Up to its joint with human shape
his crupper bunched with more serpents
than all the Maremma's swamp holds.

Between his shoulder blades, a dragon
clung with its wings spread open
setting fire to all they encountered.

My teacher said, "That is Cacus
who would fill the valley with blood
under his cave on Mt. Aventino.

He cannot run with his brothers
because of his fraudulent theft
of his neighbor's herd of oxen.

His acts of evil were finished
by Hercules' great club. He felt not
the first ten of the hundred he got."

The centaur ran past as he spoke.
Also beneath us passed three spirits
neither I nor my guide had noticed

until they yelled up, "Who are you?"
There was a break in our conversation
while we paid attention to them.

I did not know them, but it happened
as frequently it does, one let
another's name slip out, saying,

"What's holding Cianfa up?"
To get my guide to stop and listen
I held my finger to my lips.

Reader, if you are slow to believe
what I say now, it's no wonder.
I, the witness, hardly accept it.

While I stared at them, a reptile
with six legs leaped at one of them
and utterly fastened on him.

The reptile's middle feet gripped his gut,
front legs pinned the arms, and it took
the man's face between its toothed jaws.

The monster's back legs stretched down the
thighs and it snaked its tail between them,
extending back behind the loins.

Never was ivy so close rooted
to a tree as the ghastly beast
embraced those limbs with its own limbs.

Then they were melded, as if made
of molten wax; they mingled colors,
neither appearing as either's own,

as a brown color advances
before the blaze on lit paper,
not black yet while the white is going.

The other two looked, both saying,
"Agnello, look at you changing!
You are not two things or one thing!"

The two heads were becoming one
as the features of both mixed to one
face in which both faces were lost.

Four segments made couple of arms;
the legs, haunches, stomach and trunk,
became limbs never seen before.

All former form was canceled out.
The perverted image of neither
and both, slouched slowly away.

A lizard shifting hedgerows
under the long lash of the dog days
seems green lightning crossing the road:

a little reptile, flaming bright
but black as a peppercorn, made
straight for the bellies of the pair.

It bit one of them at the navel,
where our first nourishment enters,
then slipped down, splayed in front of him.

The one bitten stared at it, said
nothing. His feet stuck. He yawned, as if
overcome by sleep or fever.

He and reptile looked at each other.
Violent smoke issued from one's wound,
the other's mouth; and the smokes mixed.

Now, Lucan, let go your account
of Sabellus and Nasidius.
Wait while you hear what's to follow.

Let Ovid put aside his Cadmus
and Arethusa; one serpent, one fountain:
I don't envy his poem's changing.

He never turned natures face to face
both to their opposites, as these forms
were quick to exchange their matters.

They mirrored each other this way —
the reptile's tail became forked
while its victim's feet drew together. 160

The thighs and calves became so stuck
to each other, that their joining
quickly became invisible.

The split tail undertook the shape
the other had lost, and its skin
softened as the other's hardened.

I saw his arms sucked toward their pits,
the beast's two short legs lengthen
the length of the man's arms' shortening.

The hind legs, twisted together,
turned private member for the man
from whose distressed member two legs burst.

Meanwhile the smoke veiled both of them
with new color, depilating one,
bringing hair out on the other.

One rose, the other subsided,
though neither blinked the evil glare
under which they exchanged muzzles.

The standing one pulled excess face
up toward his temples, and issued
ears out of cheeks that had been smooth.

What was kept from flowing back there
was plenty to make a nose with
and thicken the lips as need be.

The prone thrust its muzzle forward,
retracted ears into its head
as a snail can do with its horns.

And its tongue, once a fit unit
for speech, split; and the forked end
in the other's closed as the smoke dispersed.

The spirit-become-wild-beast ran
hissing across the valley.
the other followed, spitting words;

then he turned his new back and said
to the third, "Now, Buoso can run
this road on all fours, as I have."

I saw such transformations of trash
in this seventh dump, and I trust
its novelty excuses clumsiness.

Though my eyes were confused, my mind
blurred, they were not able to run
so quickly in their disguises

I could not make out Puccio Sciancato,
who alone of three companions
I'd first seen, had not been transformed.

The last man caused Gaville's mourning.

XXVI

26

Florence, take joy that your greatness
extends across land and sea. Even
as far as hell your name is known.

Five of your citizens I found
among such thieves. This is my shame
and does Florence no great credit.

If truth shows in the morning dream
soon you will realize what Prato
and others are coveting for you.

None too soon, were it to come now:
so let it come: the older I am
the more greatly I will feel it.

We left, climbing the flight of stairs
we'd climbed down, made from the stone bridge.
My guide climbed, and gave me a hand up.

Walking our solitary path
between crags and rocks on the ridge,
we were obliged to use our hands.

When I recall what I saw there
it saddens me now as it did then,
and I restrain my invention,

that it not run beyond what's right.
If kind star or some better source
gives good strength, I'll not abuse it.

The peasant resting on the hillside
during the season when the author
of the world's light is most intimate,

as the gnats give place to mosquitos,
sees fireflies lighten in the valley
where he has plowed and gathered grapes.

With such lights the eighth trench sparkled,
I realized when I arrived
where I could look into its depth.

Like Elisha, avenged by bears,
who watched Elija's chariot
drawn into the sky by horses,

and could not follow with his eyes
except by the sight of the flame
that surrounded it like a cloud,

I saw each flame in the gulch
of the trench, not one showing its theft:
for each flame had stolen a sinner.

I leaned over the bridge edge to look,
would have fallen without a nudge
had I not caught hold of a rock.

The guide, seeing me so intent,
said, "Spirits are in those fires.
Each wraps itself in what burns it."

"Teacher," I said, "when I hear you
I'm convinced of what I had guessed,
about which I wanted to ask:

who walks in that flame whose peak is split
as if it rises from the pyre
where Eteocles burned with his brother?"

He answered, "In that are tortured
Ulysses and Diomedes,
coupled in vengeance as in anger.

They cry for the ambush of the horse
whereby Troy's gates were laid open,
and Rome's noble seed came from them.

Within their flame they mourn the trick
Deidamia mourns her Achilles for;
and suffer for robbing the temple."

"If the spirits can speak from their flames,"
I said, "I would like to beg you
with as much urging as I can,

not to refuse our waiting here
until that horned flame gets to us.
You see how I'm leaning toward it."

He said, "Your request deserves praise:
therefore I am accepting it.
But see to it you hold your tongue.

Leave the speaking to me. I'm aware
of what you wish. Since they were Greeks
they might disregard your language."

When the flame arrived beneath us,
at what seemed to my guide fit place
and time, he addressed it this way:

"Two spirits in a single fire,
I have deserved something from you
while I lived. For I wrote epic

of you while I was in the world.
Don't move, then; but, one of you, tell
where, being lost, you went to die."

The larger horn of ancient flame
began to shudder, guttering
as if harassed by wind,

and, its tip wavering back and forth
like a tongue when it is speaking,
cast a voice out that answered him,

"When I left Circe, who kept me
more than a year there near Gaeta
before Aeneas named the place,

no fondness toward my son, sympathy
for my old father, nor love owed
to making Penelope glad,

could conquer in me the great drive
I had to attain experience
of the world; human vice and value.

I set sail for the open sea
with one ship and what small crew was left
by which I'd not been deserted.

I saw all the sea's shore, from Spain
to Morocco, the isle of Sardinia,
other islands that sea washes.

My companions and I were old
and tired when we came to the strait
where Hercules placed the boundary

to keep us from attempting further.
I sailed past Seville on the right,
already passed Ceuta on the left,

and said, 'Brothers, we have reached the west
through a hundred thousand dangers.
Will you deny to the tiny

vigil remaining to your senses,
experience of what land lies
uninhabited, behind the sun?

Consider what you have come from:
you were not made to live like beasts
but to seek power and knowledge.'

This brief speech of mine so excited
my companions to the voyage
I could hardly have held them back.

So we showed our stern to the morning,
made our oars wings for the crazy flight,
veering continually southward.

Now night brought stars of the south pole,
our north star sank so low you could not
see it above the horizon.

Five waxings and five wanings of light
on the moon's under-surface passed
since we'd started the hard passage,

when a mountain appeared, hazy
with distance; a mountain so tall
I'd never seen one of such height.

We cheered. That turned to shouts of fear.
A twister, bearing down from the new
land, struck our ship fully head-on.

We made three turnings in a whirl
of sea. At the fourth, the stern rose,
the prow plowed down: another's pleasure:

until the ocean covered us."

XXVII

27

The flame, now finished, burned steady
and took itself away from us
with the kind poet's permission,

when another, coming behind it,
attracted our eyes to its peak
by the confused sound it uttered.

Like the Sicilian bull whose first
bellow was properly the scream
of the inventor who'd tuned him

to roar with the sufferer's voice
so that, even though made of brass,
it itself seemed transfixed by pain:

having at their origin no way
of exit from the flame, his words
turned into this fire's language.

But after the words made their way
to the peak, they gave it that flicker
the tongue used to begin their passage;

and we heard speech: "I direct my words
to you, who spoke Lombard just now,
saying, 'Go on, I won't keep you.'

Although I am late in coming,
please don't mind stopping to converse —
you see I don't mind; and I'm on fire.

If just now you've dropped to this blind
world from the sweet Latian country
I carried my sins from with me:

is there war or peace in Romagna?
I'm from those hills, between Urbino
and the ridge that is Tiber's source."

I stood leaning over to listen.
My guide nudged me in the side, said,
"He is a Latian. Talk to him."

My approach was already prepared.
I began without hesitation,
"Spirit hidden within the flame,

your Romagna is not, never was,
without war in its tyrants' hearts.
When I left there was no open war.

Ravenna's as it's been for years.
Polenta's eagle broods on it,
covering Cervia with its wings.

The country, after a long trial,
and bloody heaps of French, again
is under the green lion's claws.

Verrucchio's old mastiff, and his pup,
who gave Montagna bad government,
worry it with their practiced teeth.

The cities on Lamone and Santerno
a lion cub on argent field leads.
His loyalties shift with the seasons.

The town whose walls the Savio washes
where she lies between hills and flatland,
so lives between freedom, tyranny.

Now, tell us who you are: be open
with me as I was; and your name
will be made famous on the earth."

When the flame had roared in its way
a while, it flickered its sharp tip
and gave out this whispering:

"If I thought my conversation
were with one who will return to earth,
this flame would wag no longer.

But since no one returns from this depth
ever alive, I'll answer you
and not fear infamy for it.

I was soldier first, then Franciscan,
hoping the cord would make amends.
And my hope would have been fulfilled

had not the great priest, evil take him,
attracted me to my first sins.
Listen: I'll tell you how and why.

While formed of the bones and muscle
my mother gave me, my actions
were not of the lion, but the fox.

I knew all of the covert tricks
and strategies; practiced them so
their reputation was known world-wide.

When I recognized I had reached
an age when everyone ought to
take in sail, and coil his ropes down,

what I had enjoyed now grieved me.
I put myself to penitence;
and that might have been of value.

But the prince of new Pharisees
who made war from the Lateran —
and not against Jews or Saracens:

all his enemies were Christian
and not one had tried to take Acre
or done trade with the Sultan's land —

had no regard for his high office,
holy orders, nor my cincture
which once made its wearers leaner.

But as Constantine called Sylvester
to Soracte to cure his leprosy,
this one called me as the expert

to heal the fever of his pride.
He asked my counsel. I was silent;
his words seemed those of a drunk man.

Then he said, 'I absolve you now,
so your courage won't flinch later.
Teach me to crush Penestrino.

I can lock and unlock heaven
as you know, with the two keys I have.
My predecessor thought them cheap.'

The strength of the argument he made
compelled me to think silence unwise.
I said, 'Father, since you absolve me

of the sin I must undertake:
promise great things and do little.
Your throne will preside in triumph.'

When I died, St. Francis came for me,
but one of the black cherubs said,
'Don't do me wrong! Don't take this one.

He must come and join my riff-raff
for he counseled fraudulent acts.
Since that time his scalp has been mine.

What's not repented can't be absolved.
Contrition and intent don't coexist.
The contradiction precludes that.'

Poor me! How I jumped when he grabbed me
saying, 'Maybe you didn't know
that I am quite the logician!'

He carried me down to Minos
who wrapped his tail eight times around
his hard body, and bit it in rage,

said, 'Here's a bad one for the thieving
flames' — and I'm lost where you see me.
My heart's grudge walks in such clothing."

When he had completed his speech
the flame left, weeping and twisting.
Its pointed crest was still struggling.

My guide and I reached the next arch
spanning the trench where those who bet
all on a stake of divisiveness

are thrown down to collect their take.

XX
VIII

28

Even with unlimited words
and frequent tellings, who could recount
the glut of blood and wounds I saw now?

Both speech and intellect fall short,
for they have little purchase.
Therefore my telling of it fails.

Suppose one gathered all people
who ever spilled their blood over
Apulia's prosperous lands:

killed by Trojans; or in the long
war Livy faithfully recounts
produced huge booty of stripped rings;

those who suffered their wounds facing
Robert Guiscard; other people
whose quantities of bones are gathered

at Ceprano where each Apulian
proved traitor; at Tagliacozzo
where old Alardo, weaponless, won:

suppose they showed their pierced or lopped limbs,
it would not match the obscenities
that prevailed down in the ninth trench.

I saw the body of one gaped
as if stave or hoop were missing,
split from the chin to the farter.

His guts hung down between his knees;
his giblets showed, and the nasty bag
that makes shit from what it gobbles.

I was stuck staring down at him.
He stared back, pulled his chest apart
saying, "Look how I'm tearing myself.

Look how Mohammed has been maimed!
Ali goes crying in front there,
his face split from chin to forelock.

And all the others you see here,
fomenters of scandal and schism
while they lived, are split this way now.

A devil is back there, who cuts
these cruel wounds, putting each one
of this ilk to the sword again

when we complete the hard circuit,
since our wounds have closed themselves up
before we get to him again.

But who are you, up on the cliff,
to gaze around? Are you postponing
the punishment assigned to your crimes?"

"Death has not reached him, nor does guilt
bring him to torture," my guide said,
"but rather to give him full experience.

I, who have died, am to lead him
through hell, from ring to lower ring.
This is true as that I talk to you."

More than a hundred, hearing him,
stopped in the ditch to look at me,
forgetting their pain in amazement.

"Since you may see the sun shortly,
inform Fra Dolcino of this,
if he's not to follow me quickly:

to provision himself so winter
won't give the Novarese victory
they'd not easily get otherwise."

With one foot lifted to depart,
Mohammed said this to me.
His foot came down and he walked on.

Another, whose throat was slashed
and his nose trimmed back to the eyebrows,
who had a single ear remaining,

standing to gape in amazement
with the rest, opened his windpipe
(running bright red on the outside),

said, "You, whose guilt hasn't condemned you,
I've seen you in Latian country
unless similarity fools me.

Recall Pier da Medicina
if you see the sweet plain again
that slopes from Vercelli to Marcabo.

Let the two leaders in Fano,
Guido and Angiolello, know
(unless my foresight's mistaken),

they will be thrown out of their ship
weighted, drowned off Cattolica
by the treachery of a tyrant.

Between Cyprus and Majorca
the sea's not seen such a great crime
committed by Greeks or pirates.

That traitor sees out of one eye
only, and controls the country one
with me here wishes he'd never seen.

He'll invite the two to talk treaty,
then arrange that prayers to the winds
off Focara's cape, make no difference."

I said, "If you'd have me take news
back about you, show the one, explain
why his sight of that land is bitter."

Then he put his hands to the jaw
of a colleague, opened his mouth,
saying, "It's him. He doesn't speak.

This outlaw subdued Caesar's doubts,
affirming that once you're prepared
hesitation leads to ruin."

Curio: so daring in speech!
How discouraged he seemed to me,
having his tongue cut at the root!

One man with both his hands cut off
lifted their stumps to the dark air
so that his face was smeared with blood.

He said, "You'll remember Mosca,
my fatal line, 'What's done is finished,'
that sparked such harm to the Tuscans."

"And the death of your family,"
I added. His sorrow increased,
he left, frantic with his sadness.

But I stayed on to watch the crowd
and saw something I'd be afraid
even to tell, without more proof, 180

were I not bolstered by conscience.
That good companion strengthens me
in the armor of knowing it true.

I surely saw, and can still see,
a headless body walking along
like the rest of that sorry crowd.

It held its cut head by the hair,
swinging it like a lantern
that looked at us and said, "Oh, dear!"

He lifted himself along so.
He was two of one; one in two.
Only its author could explain it.

When he was right under the bridge
he raised his arm with the whole head
to bring his words closer to us,

which were, "You, breathing, visiting
the dead: look at this penalty.
See if any matches this one.

So you can take news of me back,
know that I, Bertran de Born,
gave evil advice to the young king;

made father, son, turn against each other.
Achitophel's wicked inciting
of Absalom, David, was no worse.

For separating these joined persons
I carry my brain separated
from its foundation in the body.

I am retribution's example."

XXIX

29

The crowds, and their various wounds,
had so inebriated my eyes
I wanted to stay and keep crying.

But Virgil said to me, "Why stare?
Why continue staring down there
at these sad ghosts in their maimed state?

You weren't like this at other trenches.
If you expect to count them, think:
the valley circles twenty-two miles.

Already the moon is under us.
The time allotted us is short.
There are things to see you don't see here."

"If you had given attention
to what I was studying there
you might agree we should have paused."

The guide was going on. I walked
behind him, responding to him.
I added, "Inside that cutting

I was looking into so hard,
I think a spirit of my blood
cries for the sin he's paying for."

My teacher said, "Let him stay there.
Don't let him distract your thinking.
Pay attention to other things.

I saw him, underneath the bridge,
point threateningly with his finger
at you; heard him called Geri del Bello.

You yourself were so taken up
by Altaforte's former lord
you did not look at him. He left."

"Guide," I said, "his violent death
still unavenged by anyone
associated with his shame,

made him contemptuous; so he left
without speaking to me, I expect,
and so has made me feel more for him."

We spoke this way as far as the place
where the cliff overlooked the next trench
all the way down, had there been light.

When we were at the last cloister
of Malebolge, its lay brethren
were able to be seen by us.

Various laments shot through me,
their shafts pointed with sympathy;
so I covered my ears with my hands.

Such pain there — if the hospitals
of Valdichiana, Maremma, Sardinia,
between July and September,

gathered their ill into one ditch:
as many were here. The same stench
rose up as comes from gangrenous limbs.

We went down the last escarpment
by a long rock face, still leftward,
and my view became more vivid,

toward the depth where the infallible
minister of the great Lord — justice —
punishes condemned forgers.

I think it not sadder to have seen
the people stricken in Aegina
when the air was so filled with plague

all creatures, even the smallest
worm, dropped down (and the poets say
afterwards, the ancient peoples

sprang up from ancestors of ants):
than the sight, throughout that dark valley,
of spirits in assorted heaps.

They sprawled across each other's backs,
shoulders; some were moving about
their sad road, crawling on all fours.

We picked our way without talking;
looking, listening to the sick
who could not raise their bodies up.

Two of them were sitting propped
like one pot warming another,
spotted from head to toe with scabs.

Never was currycomb so fast
scrubbed by the boy, his master waiting,
or he awake against his will,

as each spirit rapidly scratched
all over with his nails, rabid
with itching even this won't help.

So their nails scraped the scabs away
like a big knife scaling a bream
or other fish with bigger scales.

"You scaling yourself with your fingers,"
my guardian said to one of them;
"and sometimes using them like tweezers:

tell us if any Latian
is among you — and may your nails
be up to their work eternally!"

"Both of us you see rotting here
are Latians," one of them said, crying;
"But who are you to question us?"

The guide said, "I am one who descends
with this live one, from cliff to cliff,
with the aim of showing him hell."

Their mutual support dissolved.
Each, shivering, turned to face me,
with others who heard my guide speak.

My teacher looked over at me,
saying, "Say what you want of them."
I began as he suggested.

"So that your memory will not
dissipate from human attention
in the first world, but live many years,

identify your selves, your people.
Your indecent, disgusting pain
should not make you fear revealing this."

One said, "I was from Arezzo.
Albero da Siena burned me
for crime that does not place me here.

It's true I said to him, joking,
'I know how to fly through the air.'
He, having great yearning, little sense,

asked that I show him the skill. Solely
because I could not make him Daedalus
he had me burned by his father.

But to the last of these ten trenches
Minos condemned me, unerringly,
for the alchemy I practiced."

I said to the poet, "Was ever
a people vain as the Sienese?
Surely not even the French are!"

The other leper, listening,
answered my words, "Except Stricca,
who could spend so temperately!

Like Niccolo, who figured out
cloves as a main ingredient —
an example his friends followed:

the whole gang in which Caccia
d'Ascian wasted vineyard and forest,
Abbagliato showed how smart he was.

But so you will know who seconds
your opinion against the Sienese,
look hard and see my face clearly.

You'll see I'm the ghost of Capocchio
who forged metals by alchemy.
If I'm right about you, you recall

how successfully I aped nature."

XXX

30

When Juno, because of Semele,
was enraged at Thebes' royal house,
(as she demonstrated often),

she drove Athamas so insane
that, seeing his wife and two children
— one held on to each of her hands —

he yelled, "Stretch the nets at the pass,
I'll take lioness and her cubs!"
he reached his merciless clutches

grabbing the one named Learchus;
whirled him, smashed him against a rock.
She drowned herself with the other.

When fortune brought the daring pride
of the Trojans low, breaking down
both king and kingdom together,

Queen Hecuba, in misery,
captive; who'd seen Polyxena
dead; when she knew Polydorus

dead on the sea shore, was so twisted
in mind by her grief at these things
she howled like a dog in sadness.

But the furies of Thebes and Troy
never drove any so cruelly,
either beasts or human persons,

as two ghosts I saw were driven.
Naked, pale, they ran with jaws snapping
like hogs loosed out of the sty.

One rushed Capocchio, bit
the nape of his neck, threw, dragged him
so his belly scraped on the rocks.

The man from Arezzo stayed, shaking.
"That's Gianni Schicchi, rabies-crazed.
He runs around biting people."

I said, "Oh. Well, may that other one
not stick its teeth in you! Kindly
say who it is before it's gone."

He said, "That's the ancient spirit
of wicked Myrrha, who became
her father's, beyond right love, lover.

She came in false disguise like this
to indulge in sinning with him —
like Gianni Schicchi who's running off,

who impersonated Donati;
made a will, giving it legal form,
to get Donati's finest mare."   190

When both of the rabid spirits
I'd been watching had gotten past,
I turned to look the others over.

I saw one done in a lute's shape
if only his legs were cut off
crossways where a man has his crotch.

The dropsy that distorts limbs so
with lymph that won't circulate, head
and belly are out of proportion,

caused him to hold his lips open
as in the thirst of high fever:
one lip to the chin, the other up.

"Listen," he said, "you I don't know why
down here without any torture
in this awful world: pay attention

to Master Adam's misery.
Alive I had all I wanted.
Now I crave a single water drop.

Little streams coming from the green hills
of Casentino, fall to Arno,
make their beds cool and moisten them.

I see them all the time, and with reason,
for their image dessicates me
worse than the illness I waste from.

The stern justice that ransacks me
takes its tool from the place I sinned
to put more wind in my sighing.

I see Romena, where I made
counterfeit coin with St. John's seal.
For this I had my body burnt up there.

I'd not trade the spring at Branda
for sight of those rotten spirits, here,
of Guido, Alessandro, their brother.

One's inside now, if the raging
muddle of ghosts is telling the truth:
but what good's that to me, immobile?

If I were only that much lighter
I could move an inch a century
I'd be on my way already

to search him out in this obscene
crowd, though it circles eleven miles,
and never's less than a mile across.

It's their fault I'm in this shit family.
They induced me to stamp as pure, gold
coins that were three carats base metal."

I said, "Who are the two wastrels
steaming like washed hands in the winter
lying up close to your right side?"

"When I rained into this trench," he said,
"I found them here. Since then they've not
turned over once; and won't forever.

The woman accused Joseph falsely.
The man's Sinon, false Greek of Troy.
High fever makes them reek so much."

The latter, perhaps insulted
at this dubious introduction,
smacked his fist on Adam's stretched belly

that gave out the sound of a drum.
Master Adam punched him in the face
with an arm equally swollen,

saying, "Maybe the weight of my limbs
completely keeps me from moving;
but I've got an arm free for this."

Sinon said, "Your arms weren't so free
when you were walking to the fire —
but freer at counterfeiting."

The dropsical: "You speak the truth.
But you weren't so true a witness
when Trojans asked the truth of you."

"If I spoke false, you coined falsehood,"
Sinon said. "I'm here for one crime;
you for more than any devil."

"Remember the wooden horse, perjurer,"
the one with distended guts said,
"so suffer! The whole world knows it!"

"You suffer," said the Greek, "the thirst
that cracks your tongue; the putrid liquid
that crowds your eyes out with belly."

The counterfeiter: "As usual
your mouth cracks open on bad talk.
So I'm thirsty and stuffed with lymph!

You're burning up, and your head hurts,
and you'd not need much inviting
to lap Narcissus' looking-pool."

I was so stuck listening to them
my teacher said, "Keep on staring
much longer, and we'll be at odds."

When I sensed his anger with me
I turned back to him in such shame
remembering it still shames me.

I wished to be excused, and was
excused, not thinking myself so;
not able even to speak my wish —

like a person dreaming some harm
who dreams, "I wish this were a dream,"
wishing what is as if it were not.

My teacher said, "Less shame absolves
worse faults than yours was. So disburden
yourself of all this contrition,

and depend on my company
should fortune again bring you to
people in similar disputes.

It is a low wish to overhear."

XXXI

31

This single speech both scolded me
so that both my cheeks colored,
and extended cure for the hurt.

I've heard the spear of Achilles
and his father was the cause first
of painful, then of healing gift.

We gave our backs to that sorry trench
without talking, climbing the bank
that serves as the ravine's girdle.

Here was dusk between night and day.
I could barely see in front of me,
but I heard a deep horn sounding

loud enough to make thunder seem soft.
Following the sound toward its source,
my eyes searched for where it came from.

The ring of Roland's horn, Charlemagne's
holy enterprise lost in slaughter,
did not sound such terrible signal.

After looking that way a while
I thought I saw many high towers,
and said, "Teacher, what is this town?"

He said, "Because you try to see
through so long a stretch of darkness,
imagination leads you off.

When we get there, you will recongize
how distance distorts your senses —
and so you should push yourself on."

He grabbed my hand encouragingly,
said, "Before you have gone farther,
so the real will seem less unlikely,

you should know those are not towers,
but giants, up to their middles
in the pit, the whole way around."

When a fog unravels, one's vision
little by little reformulates
what the mist-filled air had hidden.

So, boring through this thick, dark air,
the closer we got to the edge
my mistake decreased, and fear grew.

It was like the circular wall
crowned with towers at Montereggione:
the bank surrounding this ravine

had turrets of the upper halves
of awful giants. Jupiter
still threatens them when he thunders.

I could already make out the face,
chest, shoulders, most of the stomach,
of one — and his arms at both sides.

When nature abandoned the craft
of making these beasts, she did well
to strip warfare of such agents.

If you think of it carefully,
you'll find it fair and moderate
she did not withdraw whales, elephants:

for where the techniques of mind
join power and the will to evil,
people have no defense from it.

His face was as huge and as rough
as St. Peter's big bronze pinecone,
and his limbs were in proportion.

The embarkment was his apron
waist down; and so much showed above
three Friesians on each other'd boast

in vain they could reach to his hair:
for it was a good thirty feet
from his waist to where your cloak's clasped.

"Shlog poona carcle flum hox!"
his wild mouth started in yelling —
mouth fit for such charming psalm songs.

My guide said to him, "Stupid spirit,
stick to your horn. Let that express you
when you're angry or otherwise moved.

If you look round your neck, you'll find
the thong it is tied on, idiot!
And the horn is lying on your chest."

Then my guide told me, "It is himself
he is mad at; Nimrod, whose dumb plan
led to the world's babel of language.

Let's leave him be; not waste our talk.
Every single language to him is
like his language, that is known to none."

So we extended our journey,
veering leftward; a bowshot's length
on was the next one, bigger, fiercer.

I don't know who was strong enough
to chain him. His left arm was fastened
in front; his right in back of him,

by a chain that from the neck down
bound him. What I could see of him
was wrapped five times around with chain.

"This one had the conceit to pit
his strength against that of Jupiter,"
said my guide. "Here is his reward.

He is named Ephialtes. Big doings
when giants made the gods tremble.
He waved his arms then, but not now."

I said, "I'd like, if I could, to see
Briareus the Immeasurable,
so my eyes could have that experience."

He answered, "You will see Antaeus.
He's nearer. He talks, and is not tied.
He'll set us down in all evil's pit.

The one you want to see is much further.
He is tied up, made like this one,
but he is fiercer in the face."

Never was tower so shaken
by the most robust of earthquakes,
as Epiphialtes shook suddenly.

I was more afraid of dying
now than ever. Fear would have done it
if I had not seen his shackles.

And so we proceeded along,
came to Antaeus' good fifty yards
(not counting the head) above the trench.

"You took a thousand lions once
in the same auspicious valley
where the retreat of Hannibal

left Scipio to his triumph.
Had you joined with your brothers' war,
you children of earth might have won —

at least there are those who think so.
Don't be fastidious. Reach us down
to where the cold locks Cocytus.

Don't make us try Typhon or Tityus.
This person can give what you want here,
so lean down and stop your sneering:

he can restore your fame in the world.
He lives, and expects a long life
unless grace calls him to her first,"

my teacher said. Antaeus quickly
reached with those hands Hercules felt
clenching, and took up my guardian.

Virgil, when he felt himself lifted,
said, "Get where I can hold on to you
and make one lot of both of us."

When a cloud passes behind it
and you look from its leaning side
upward, the tower seems to be falling.

Antaeus bending looked like that.
It was so awful I wanted
any other way to go down.

He reached us lightly to depth devouring
Lucifer and Judas together,
didn't stay long bending over,

but rose like the mast of a ship.

XXXII

32

If I had lines harsh and choking
enough to fit the sorry hole
the other rock terraces lean on,

I would squeeze the fullest essence
from my conceit. Not having them,
I'm diffident to talk of it.

It's nothing to fool with, describing
the pit of the whole universe
with mamma dadda baby talk.

Ladies, come help with my verses;
you helped Amphion wall Thebes in.
Keep my words true to what happened.

Oh, you'd been better off as goats
or sheep here, you badly-made riff-raff,
than in that place it's hard to talk of.

Now we were down in the dark pit,
deeper than the giant's feet were.
I was still staring at the high wall,

heard talking: "Watch your step! Look out
you don't trample on your brothers
miserable heads with your feet!"

At this I looked down, saw at my feet
and extending out, a lake. Ice
gave it the look of glass, not water.

The Danube in Austria; Don
way up under the polar sky,
never veiled their rush so thickly

as here: should mountain giant fall
(Tambernic, Pietrepana), on its face,
not even its edge would crackle.

While country women think gleaning,
frogs sit in the water, their noses
poked above it, to let them croak.

Colorless up to their shamed blushes,
ghosts frozen into the lake cried.
Their teeth clacked together like storks' beaks.

Each of them kept the face bent down.
Their chattering witnessed the cold;
their eyes witnessed their sullen hearts.

When I had looked around awhile
I saw two at my feet so close
on each other their hair was tangled.

"You with your chests mashed together,"
I said, "who are you?" They bent up
their necks so their faces faced me.

Their eyes, first only wet inside,
trickled their lids apart. The freeze
clutched their tears, shut their lids again.

Clamps don't hold wood to wood tighter.
So much rage came on them they butted
each other like two billy goats.

Another one who'd lost both ears
to frostbite, said, his head still down,
"Why do you stare at us so much?

So you want to know who those two are?
The whole Bisenzio valley
was theirs, and their father Albert's.

They came out of one body. Search
all Caina, you'll not find a ghost
who deserves more to be stuck in aspic:

not that one - Mordred - his chest and ghost
Arthur's spear cracked at the same time:
not feuding Focaccia: not him

with the head there that blocks my view,
Sassol, who murdered his brother
to get the full inheritance.

So you don't force me to talk more,
I'm Camicion, cousin-killer.
Carlin's treachery will make mine pale."

I saw a thousand more faces
the cold made as surly as dogs. Always
when I see frozen pond now, I shake.

While we were walking toward the middle
where the weight of all things comes together
(I shivered from the eternal shade) —

whether destiny, will, or chance
caused it, walking amongst the heads,
I stubbed my foot hard on a face.

The face screeched, "Why did you kick me?
unless you're here for vengeance
on account of Montaperti?"

I said, "Teacher, please wait for me
while he resolves a question of mine;
then hurry me as much as you want."

The guide stopped. I said to the face
still cursing lustily along,
"Who are you to complain of others?"

"No! Who are you to kick someone's head
harder than if you were live man,
when you travel this traitors' lake?"

"Live man I am," I said, "with power
precious to you. If you want fame
I'll add your name to the well-known."

He said, "I long for the reverse.
Get out! Don't give me more trouble.
Your flattery's no good in this stretch."

So I jerked him up by the scalp,
said, "You'd better give me your name,
or I'll not leave a hair on you."

He said, "You can yank my hair out
and give my head a thousand kicks.
I won't tell or show who I am."

I'd got his hair twisted around
my hand, already pulled some hunks out;
he still kept his eyes down, and yelped;

when another shouted, "Hey, Bocca!
Your tooth music's not enough; you bark
too? What devil's poking at you?"

"Now I won't need your story," I said,
"you damned traitor! I'll carry the news
of you up there. Truth is your shame!"

"Go on," he said, "tell what you want;
but the one that just used his big mouth —
if you get out, don't keep him secret.

He's crying about that French bribe.
You can say, 'I saw Buoso da Duera
where sinners are kept in cold storage.'

If they ask you who else was there,
you've got Beccheria beside you,
whose throat Florence had cut for him.

Farther on's Gianni de Soldanier
with Ganelon, and Tribaldello
who opened sleeping Faenza."

We'd already left him. I saw
two ghosts frozen into one hole,
the head of one capping the other.

The famished gnaws a loaf of bread.
The upper one chewed the other's head
and neck, at the base of the brain.

Tydeus, in his great rage, gnawed
at Menalippus' head, the way
this one chewed the skull and whatnot.

"You, showing such a bestial proof
of hatred of whom you're eating,
tell me the reason," I said, "and I,

if you have cause for your complaint,
knowing who you are, and his crime,
will pay you back up in the world,

if what I'm talking with survives this."

XXXIII

33

The sinner lifted his mouth off
the violent meal, wiped his lips
on the head's hair, what was left of it.

He started, "What you're asking me
is to revive desperate grief,
heart-wrenching in thought, worse to speak.

But maybe my words can be seeds
to fruit infamy for this traitor
I gnaw. I'll talk while I'm crying.

I don't know who you are, nor how
you came down here; but hearing you
I think you are really from Florence.

You should know I am Count Ugolino.
This other's Archbishop Ruggieri.
Listen why I'm this kind of neighbor.

I don't have to say, by his schemes,
putting my confidence in him,
I was taken, then put to death.

Here is what you cannot have heard:
how cruel my death was. Listen,
and decide if he has hurt me.

In the prison is a narrow cell
named 'Starvation' because of me.
Others will still be locked in there.

I'd already seen several moons
from its window slit, when I slept
nightmare that unveiled the future.

I dreamed what seemed to be a lord
hunting wolf and its cubs on the mountain
that blocks Lucca from Pisa's view.

His hounds lean, attentive, clever,
he had Gualandi for company,
with Sismondi and Lanfranchi.

After short run, the father wolf
and sons tired; and the dogs' sharp teeth,
it seemed, were ripping at their flanks.

I woke before dawn, heard my sons
and their sons, who were with me, crying
in their sleep, and begging for bread.

If you're not grieved already, thinking
of what was in my heart, you are cruel.
If you don't cry now, what will make you?

Now they woke. It was about time
when they usually brought us food.
Everyone's dream made him worried. 210

Then I heard them nail up the door
at the foot of our tower prison.
I looked at the boys without speaking.

I did not cry; hardened inside.
They cried. My little Anselm said,
'Father, what makes you look like that?'

But I did not cry, or answer
all through the day, or the next night,
till sun rose on the world again.

When a small ray of sun entered
the cell of sadness, I made out
four faces that wore my despair.

From grief I started biting my hands.
They, thinking I did that from urge
of hunger, suddenly jumped up,

said, 'Father, it would give us less pain
if you eat from us. You clothed us
in this poor flesh: you take it off!'

I calmed down, not to make them sadder.
That day and the next we kept silence.
Why could earth not gape open for us?

When we had come to the fourth day,
Gaddo threw himself at my feet
saying, 'Father, why can't you help me?'

He died there. As sure as you see me,
I saw the next three fall one by one
on the fifth and sixth days. Then blind,

I took to groping amongst them,
calling them two days after they died.
After — starvation conquered grief."

He said this, and then his eyes bulged,
he grabbed at that sorry skull again,
mumbled the bone with strong dog teeth.

Ah, Pisa! scandal to the lovely
country where we speak "yes" with "si,"
since your neighbors are slow to revenge;

let isles Capraia and Gorgona
slide in to dam the Arno's mouth
so every living soul there drowns!

Even if Count Ugolino
betrayed your fortress away,
you should not have tortured the children!

Pisa, new Thebes! Their young ages
made little Ugo, and Brigata,
innocent as the two boys I named.

We walked onward to where the ice
tightly encases more people,
these facing upward, rather than down.

Their very tears block their letting
tears; and crying, finding their eyes stopped,
works inward to increase their pain.

For their very first tears harden
and fill, like visors of crystal,
all the hollow below the eyebrow.

It seemed to me I was feeling wind,
even though cold had caused my face
to lose all feeling, as if callous

had grown over it. So I said,
"Teacher, what can make this wind move?
Is not all transpiration stopped here?" 212

He said, "Soon you will be where your own
eyes can answer, seeing the source
from which the wind is generated."

Then a rascal in the cold crust
called to us, "Spirits so cruel
the deepest spot's assigned to you,

lift the hard film from my eyelids
to release the grief that's backed up
in my heart, before they freeze again."

I said, "If you want me to help you,
say who you are. Then if I don't
clear your eyes, may I be locked in ice."

So he said, "I'm Brother Alberic.
I had my friend killed with his son
at the fruit course — here's my dessert!"

"My," I said, "are you dead already?"
and he said, "How my body may be
up in the world, I have no idea.

Ptolemy's ice-yard has this chance:
that often the spirit falls here
before Lady Death squeezes it out.

And to encourage you lifting
the glazing of tears from my face,
listen: when the spirit turns traitor

as I did, its body's taken
by a demon, which directs it
until its time has been filled out.

The spirit falls to this cistern.
It may be the body's still up there
of that ghost wintering behind me.

You should know if you just came down.
He's Branca d'Oria. Many years
have passed since he was frozen in."

"I think you're fooling me," I said.
"Branca d'Oria's never died.
He eats, drinks, sleeps, puts his clothes on."

"When Branca killed Michel Zanche,
at the same moment Zanche's spirit
fell to the Malebranchers' pitch pot,

a demon took his spirit's place
in his body; and that of his kin
who joined him in the treachery.

Stretch your hand out now; open my eyes."
I wouldn't do it. Courtesy
demanded this discourtesy.

Oh, you Genoese! removed entirely
from all propiety, corruption-
filled! Why aren't you cast out of the world?

Look! With Romagna's worst spirit
I found your Branca's ghost in hell
for his crimes, even at this time

while his body seems alive up here.

XXXIV

34

Vexilla regis prodeunt inferni

"Behold the banners of the Lord
of hell advance: look out ahead!
See if you make him out," my guide said.

Now, through the wafting of thick mist,
or when night grows on our hemisphere,
a windmill's seen turning from far off.

I thought I saw such a structure.
I crept back behind my guardian,
for there was no other windbreak.

I'd come (I'm afraid to put it
in verse), where the ghosts were quite buried.
You could see them, like specks in glass.

Some lay about; some were erect:
one head up, and one upside down,
one bent like a bow face to feet.

We had advanced far enough now,
and my teacher was pleased to show me
Lucifer, who was once lovely.

He stepped from in front of me, held me,
said, "Look at Satan, and his place!
You must steel yourself with fortitude."

Reader, don't ask — I don't write it —
how frozen faint I became then.
No number of words would suffice.

I neither died nor stayed living.
If you can imagine, try to:
being deprived of both conditions.

The emperor of this sad kingdom
issued waist-up out of the ice.
I'm closer to a giant in size

than giant's would be to his arms.
Now think how big the whole thing is
in proportion to that one part.

If he was beautiful as ugly
now, and could despise his maker,
well might he be source of all mourning.

I saw what greatly amazed me:
there were three faces on his head.
One was in front, and vermilion.

The other two were joined to it
from the crest of his skull right down
to the center of each shoulder.

The right one was yellowish white,
the left was, when you looked at it,
like faces from where the Nile falls.

Under each head, two huge wings sprouted,
the right size for so large a bird.
I never saw sails that big at sea.

They weren't feathered, but of a bat's
style; and he was beating with them
so three winds moved away from him.

It's these winds that froze Cocytus.
He cried from his six eyes; three chins
drooled with tears and a bloody foam. 218

His teeth, like hackles, were shredding
a sinner in each of his mouths —
so he kept all three suffering.

For the one in front, the biting
was nothing compared to the chewing.
The skin was flayed right off his back.

"The spirit up there who has worst pain,"
my guide said, "is Judas Iscariot,
with his head inside, his legs kicking.

The two whose heads hang down and out:
Brutus dangles from the black's mouth —
look how he twists, speaks not a word —

that's Cassius who looks so brawny.
But night comes on now. It is time
to push on. We've seen everything."

I clasped his neck as he directed,
and he watched for an opening
and, when the wings were extended

he took hold of the shaggy side,
lowered us down from tuft to tuft,
between matted hair and crust ice.

When we'd come where the hip sockets,
where there's that curving in the haunch,
my guide, fatigued, and with some trouble,

turned his head where his feet had been,
grabbed on the hair like someone climbing.
I thought we were heading back down in.

"Hold on! This is the kind of stairs
we use to get out of such evil,"
my guide said, panting in exhaustion.

Then we came out at a rock cleft
and he settled me on its brink,
and carefully climbed after me.

I looked up where we'd come from, thinking
to see Lucifer as I'd left him:
saw his legs — he was upside down.

I was as confused as anyone
too thick to figure out what point
my teacher and I had passed through.

"Get to your feet," my teacher said.
It's a long and a hard track still.
The sun's halfway through morning prayers."

Where we stood was no castle hall,
but a natural stone dungeon,
treacherous underfoot, and dark.

When I'd stood up, I said, "Teacher,
before we get out of the abyss,
say something to correct my mistakes.

Where is this glacier? How's he stuck
upside down that way? How's the sun
crossed so fast from night to morning?"

"You think you're on the center's far side,
where I grabbed the hair of that worm
who's drilled the world with evil," he said.

"That was true while I climbed downward.
When I turned, we passed the mid-point
which attracts the weight of all things.

You've arrived under the hemisphere
opposite the one dry land covers,
beneath whose central peak was killed 220

one born, and who lived, without sin.
Your feet are on a little sphere,
the other face of the Judas hole.

Here's morning while it's evening there.
The one whose fur we were climbing
is still stuck there as he first was.

He fell from heaven on this side
on land that first had been convex,
but drew in from fear, left veil of sea

while it pushed up to our hemisphere.
What land you see here, perhaps rose
to escape him, leaving that hole."

At the far end of Satan's tomb,
invisible in the darkness —
but you can hear it from its sound —

is little stream running down there,
through the rock cavern it's worn away.
Its course winds in a mild descent.

By this hidden route my guide and I
commenced our return to open world.
Not bothering to take a rest,

we climbed, he leading, I behind;
until, through a round gap, I glimpsed
lovely things that heaven carries.

We came out: again saw the stars.

Glossary

There follows a list, with some descriptive additions, of people and places mentioned by name in the *Inferno,* excluding those which are contained in the *American Heritage Dictionary* (New College Edition). At the end of each entry, in parenthesis, is the number of the canto in which the name appears. In some cases an individual is referred to indirectly, and not by name. In such cases, the most likely clue has been chosen from the text, and listed below, with the full identity attached. Thus Griffolino of Arezzo, identified in the text only by his own speech "I was from Arezzo," is listed under *Arezzo.*

Abbagliato. A member of the Spendthrift Club of Siena, Bartolomeo dei Folcaccieri, was nicknamed Abbagliato, or Muddlehead. (29)

Achitophel. The *Book of Samuel* recounts the story of Achitophel's inciting Absalom to revolt against his father, King David. (28)

Adam, Master. A counterfeiter, put to death in 1281, in Florence. The lords of Romena had encouraged him in this crime. (30)

Aegina. One of the isles of Greece, location for the myth, recounted in Ovid's *Metamorphoses,* of a plague that killed all but one of the inhabitants, Aeacus, who prayed to Jupiter and, in answer to his prayer, saw the island's ants transformed to humans. (29)

Agnello. A Florentine thief. (25)

Alardo. Erard de Valery, in 1268, assisted Charles of Anjou to victory at the battle of Tagliacozzo. (28)

Alberic, Brother. Alberigo, of the Manfredi family, had his brother Manfred, together with Manfred's son, murdered at the banquet to which Alberigo had invited them in his own home, in 1284. (33)

Albero da Siena. A powerful fool who, disappointed at the failure of Griffolino da Arezzo to teach him to fly, caused him to be burned at the stake for the practice of magic. (29)

Albert. Count Alberto of Mangona's two sons, Napoleone and Alessandro degli Alberti, killed each other while struggling over their inheritance. (32)

Alessandro (da Romena). One of the Conti Guidi (the others are Guido, Aghinolfo, and Ildebrando) who encouraged Master Adam in his crime of counterfeiting. (30)

Alessio Interminei. A member of a worthy family from Lucca. (18)

Ali. Ali, the son-in-law of Mohammed, was Caliph after him from 656 until his assassination in 661. (28)

Altaforte's former lord. See Bertran de Born.

Amphiaraus. One of the seven kings who fought against Thebes, Amphiaraus of Argos was swallowed up by the earth. (20)

Anastasius, Pope. Pope Anastasius II (pope for two years, 496-498) was confused by Dante with Emperor Anastasius (491-518), who embraced Photinus' heresy. (11)

Angiolello. Angiolello da Carignano, invited with Guido del Cassero to a conference by Malatestino of Rimini ("he who sees out of one eye only"); the two were drowned by Malatestino as a part of his campaign to secure their town Fano for himself. (28)

Anselm(uccio). Grandson of Ugolino, and murdered with him. (33)

Arezzo - "I was from Arezzo...". The speaker who identifies himself thus is Griffolino of Arezzo. (See Albero da Siena.)

Arrigo. A citizen of Florence. (6)

Aruns. This Etruscan haruspex prophesied Caesar's victory over Pompey. (20)

Asdente. A cobbler from Parma, who prophesied in the late 13th century. (20)

Athamas. Juno, enraged over her husband Jupiter's infidelity with the mortal woman Semele (by which union Bacchus was produced) took revenge on the entire royal house of Thebes. She tricked Semele into encountering Jupiter in his godly aspect (which destroyed her); and she drove Athamas, husband of Semele's sister Ino, insane, such that he was responsible for the deaths of his wife and children. (30)

Azzolino. Ezzolino III da Romano (1194-1259), head of the Ghibelline party in Northern Italy, was a tyrant of renowned cruelty. (12)

Beatrice. Born in 1266, the daughter of Folco Portinari, Beatrice married Simone dei Bardi, and died in 1290. Dante's attraction to and admiration for her led him to assign to Beatrice the role of spiritual guide. (2)

Beccheria. Tesauro dei Beccheria of Pavia, the Abbot of Vallambrosa and a papal legate for Alexander IV in Florence, was killed in 1258 by the Guelphs of Florence, on account of his interaction with the exiled Ghibellines. (32)

Benaco, Lake. Now known as Lake Garda.

Bertran de Born. The Provencal troubadour Bertran de Born was supposed to have encouraged Prince Henry ("the young king") to revolt against his father, Henry II of England. (28)

Bisenzio. Italian river near Florence, a tributary of the Arno. (32)

Bocca. Bocca degli Abati pretended to side with the Guelphs of Florence, but, his sympathies actually with the Ghibellines of Siena, he cut down the Guelph standard at the battle of Montaperti (1260), leading to their defeat.

Boniface. Pope Boniface VIII (1217-1303) is expected by Pope Nicholas III, who, from his flaming pit, addresses Dante as Boniface. Nicholas further predicts the advent of Clement V ("lawless shepherd of ugly works"). (19)

Bonturo. Bonturo Dati, an official from Lucca, well known for graft. The phrase "except Bonturo" is a joke. He was exiled from Lucca in 1314. (21)

Branca D'Oria. Branca D'Oria murdered Michel Zanche, his father-in-law, at a dinner to which Branca had invited him. Branca died in 1325, his

soul having long since taken its place in Ptolomea. (33)
Brigata. A grandson of Ugolino, and murdered with him. (33)
Brunetto Latini. Florentine politician and author of the *Tesoro,* (1220-1294), whose work Dante greatly admired. (15).
Bulicame. A hot spring near Viterbo. (14)
Buoso. A thief. (25)
Caccia d'Ascian. A member of the Spendthrifts Club of Siena. (29)
Cacus. The centaur Cacus, a son of Vulcan, lived in a cave under Mount Aventino. He stole cattle from Hercules, who took revenge by killing him. (25)
Cain-in-the-moon. The man-in-the-moon, with his thornbush (as Shakespeare saw him), is here given the name of Cain, the first murderer, after whom a part of hell is named. (20, 5, 32)
Camicion (de' Pazzi). Camicion murdered a kinsman, Ubertino.
Camilla. Camilla, as the *Aeneid* recounts, was a warrior princess killed while defending her country from the invading Trojans. (1)
Capaneus. Capaneus, one of the seven kings who besieged Thebes, was killed there during the assault, in the act of blaspheming against Jupiter. (14)
Capocchio. Capocchio (perhaps a nickname) was burned for alchemy in Siena in 1293. (29)
Capraia. An island positioned near the mouth of the Arno River. (33)
Caprona. A fortress of Pisa, captured by the Tuscan Guelphs in 1289, an operation in which Dante appears to have taken part. (21)
Cardinal, The. Cardinal Ottaviano degli Ubaldini, 1210-1273. (10)
Carlin. Carlino de' Pazzi, a relative of Camicion (above), who, in 1302, accepted a bribe to betray the castle of Piantravigne to the Black party of Florence. (32)
Casalodi, (Alberto da). Alberto da Casalodi, the lord of Mantua, was advised by Pinamonte de Buonaccorsi to banish the important nobles of Mantua. This done, Pinamonte led the populace in a massacre of the remaining families of note, exiled Count Albert, and himself took over the city. (20)
Casentino. A district in Tuscany which waters the Arno. (30)
Catalano, Brother. A member of the *Frati Gaudenti* he, together with Loderingo degli Andolo, was in 1266 appointed to the office of *Podesta* in Florence. The Gardingo was a part of Florence. (23)
Cattolica. Italian town on the Adriatic. (28)
Ceprano. The pass of Ceprano, near the town of that name, was the site of a battle in which the barons of Apulia, entrusted by Manfred with the defense of the pass, traitorously allowed the advance of Charles of Anjou, 1266. (28)
Cervia. A town near Ravenna, some twelve miles south. (27)
Charles. Charles d'Anjou, 1220-1284, king of Naples and Sicily. Son of Louis VIII of France, his entrance into Italy, and assumption of the crown of Naples, were attended by much intrigue, involving Pope Urban IV,

Clement IV, and Nicholas III, who turned against him in response to a bribe from the Emperor Palaeologus. (19, 28)
Cianfa (de Donati). A thief of Florence. (25)
Cornelia. Mother of the Gracchi (the Tribunes Tiberius and Caius), Cornelia was regarded by the Roman civilization as the exemplar of motherhood. (4)
Corneto. The Maremma, a swampy district of Tuscany, is bordered by the rivers Cecina and Marte, on whose banks the town of Corneto sits. The Maremma was renowned for endemic fevers. (13)
Council of the Jews. Caiaphas and his father-in-law Annas were among those responsible for the judgement that Jesus should suffer execution. (23)
Curio. (Caius Cribonius). Tribune of the Plebs, in 50 B.C., was supposed to have advised Julius Caesar to cross the Rubicon, the boundary whose crossing was in act equivalent to a declaration of war against the republic of Rome. (28)
Deidamia. Deidamia, after bearing Achilles a child, died of grief when Achilles left her, encouraged to do so by Ulysses. (26)
Dejanira. The centaur Nessus was shot by Hercules while Nessus was attempting to rape Dejanira, Hercules' wife. Nessus gave Dejanira a cloak, soaked in the blood of this mortal wound, telling Dejanira that if Hercules wore it, his love for Dejanira would be preserved. The cloak instead caused the death of Hercules; and Dejanira killed herself. (12)
Diascorides. Author of *De Materia Medica,* a treatise on the medical properties of plants, a Greek scientist of the first century A.D. (4)
Dis. The underworld of Greek mythology; the city of Dis enclosed the inner circles of Dante's hell. (8)
Donati, (Buoso). Buoso Donati having died, his son Simone, hiding his father's death, hired Gianni Schicchi to impersonate the dead man, in order to alter the will. Schicchi took advantage of the situation by willing himself the dead man's best mare. (30)
Duke of Athens. Theseus, the hero of Greek mythology. (12)
Empedocles. Greek philosopher, 5th century B.C. (4)
Ephialtes. A giant, son of Neptune and Iphimedia, he attempted to pile Mt. Pelion on Ossa in order to make a way for the giants to ascend to heaven, and was against the gods. (31)
Erichto. This Thessalian witch, mentioned by Lucan, was said to bring souls back to their dead bodies. No source has been found for the story of Virgil's travel through hell. (9)
Eteocles. Eteocles and his brother Polynices, the sons of Oedipus and Jocasta, killed each other in combat over the succession to Thebes. They were burned on the same funeral pyre. (26)
Euryalus. Trojan warrior, companion of Aeneas. (1)
Eurypylus. During the Trojan War, Euryalus was the augur who, with Calchas, was asked to determine the best time for the Greeks to put to sea in order to launch their attack. (20)

Fano. See Angiolello.
Farinata (degli Uberti). Florentine leader of the Ghibelline party, died in 1264; a heretic. (6, 10)
Filippo Argenti. (The Weeper), a member of the Adimari family. Dante's special hatred for this Florentine has not been explained. (8)
Flegias. Son of Mars, Flegias burned the temple of Apollo, enraged at Apollo's rape of his daughter. Apollo killed him. He is here seen as the patron of the wrathful. (8)
Focaccia. A memeber of the Cancellieri family of Pistoia, he murdered his cousin Detto de' Cancellieri through treachery. (32)
Fra Dolcino. Fra Dolcino's "Apostolic Brothers", after Pope Clement V ordered their dissolution in 1305, hid in the hills near Novara, but were besieged by the forces of the pope, and overcome by starvation. Dolcino was burned at the stake in 1307. (28)
France, King of. Philip IV (le Bel), 1285-1314), with whom Pope Clement V, "lawless shepherd of ugly works", indulged in intrigue, even to moving the papal seat from Rome to Avignon. (19)
Francesca. Francesca da Rimini, married to Gianciotta da Verruchio, accepted his brother Paolo Malatesta as her lover. Gianciotta murdered them together when he surprised them coupled, as they remain in hell. (5)
Francesco D'Accorso. Lawyer from Florence, 1225-1293. (15)
Frederick. Emperor Frederick II, 1194-1250, supposed to have been an Epicurean; patron of Pier delle Vigne, who committed suicide after he fell from favor; and supposed to have invented cloaks of lead which were melted while being worn by those condemned as traitors. (10, 13, 23)
Gaddo. Son of Ugolino, and murdered with him. (33)
Galahad. Because Galahad acted as intermediary for Lancelot and Guinevere, his name is used as synonymous with that role. (5)
Ganelon. In the *Chanson de Roland,* Roland, the nephew of Charlemagne, is betrayed and delivered over to the Saracens (along with the rest of the rear guard which he commands) by Ganelon, his father-in-law. (32)
Gardingo. See Catalano.
Gaville. "The last man caused Gaville's mourning". This is Francesco de Cavalcanti. He was killed by the inhabitants of Gaville, a village on the Arno, and his kinsmen later took severe revenge on the townspeople. (25)
Geri del Bello. A kinsman of Dante's family, his murder had apparently not been avenged by the Alighieri in 1300, as the custom of blood feud required. (29)
Ghisola(bella). Venedico Caccianemico (b. 1228) was accused of prostituting his sister Ghisolabella to the Marquis of Este (either Obizzo II, or Azzo, his son). (18)
Giacomo da Sant'Andrea. Giacomo, from Padua, and Lano, probably

from Siena, are profligates. Lano, who had squandered his fortune, remained to die at the battle of Toppo (121), when he might have escaped. (13)

Gianfigliazzi. A family of usurers from Florence, represented here by their coat of arms. (17)

Gianni Schicchi. See Donati.

Gianni de Soldanier. A Florentine who deserted the Ghibelline party and joined the Guelphs. (32)

Gomita, Brother. Brother Gomita from Gallura was chancellor for Nino Visconti, Governor of Pisa; and in that position Gomita sold public offices and took bribes to allow the escape of prisoners. Nino had him executed for his crimes. (22)

Gorgona. An island near the Arno's mouth. (33)

Green lion. Sinibaldo degli Ordelaffi, tyrant of Forli. (27)

Gualandi. A leading Pisan family of the Ghibelline party. (33)

Gualdrada. A real woman who, for her beauty, intelligence, and her modesty, had become legend by the time Dante wrote. Her grandson, Guido Guerra (1220-1272), was a leader in the Guelph party, who had advised his party against the disastrous campaign against Siena in 1260. (16)

Guglielmo Borsiere. According to Boccaccio, a matchmaker, peacemaker, and courtier. (16)

Guido (Cavalcanti). The son of Cavalcante dei Cavalcante (1255-1300) who asks after his well-being from his heretic's tomb, a poet and Dante's close friend. (10)

Giudo Bonatti. Astrologer from Forli, who was employed by Guido da Montefeltro. (20)

Guido (da Roma). See Alessandro. (30)

Guido (del Cassero). See Angiolello. (28)

Guido Guerra. See Gualdrada. (16)

Holy face. An image of Christ in the church of San Martino, in Lucca. (21)

Hypsipyle. When the women of Lemnos killed all the men on the island, Hypsipyle saved her father, king Thoas. Jason seduced and betrayed her. (18)

Jacopo Rusticucci. Florentine politician, whose fate among the sodomites is blamed on his wife's temper. (6, 16)

Jehosaphat. A valley in Israel which, by Old Testament tradition, was expected to be the site of the last judgement. (10)

Joseph. "The woman who accused Joseph falsely" is the wife of the Egyptian counselor Potiphar, who accused Joseph of responsibility for her own attempt to seduce him. (30)

Julia. Daughter of Julius Caesar, and wife of Pompey. (4) Lanfranchi. Important Pisan family of the Ghibelline party. (33)

Lano. See Giacomo da Sant'Andrea. (13)

Latium. The central region of Italy, within which Rome was founded

as recorded in Virgil's *Aeneid.* The King of Latium (4) is Latinus, from whom Aeneas conquered the country in mythological times.
Lavinia. Daughter of King Latinus, delivered to Aeneas in marriage at the conclusion of Aeneas' war of conquest. (4)
Learchus. Son of Athamas. (see Athamas) (30)
Lion cub on argent field. Mainardo Pagano, lord of Faenza (represented by his coat of arms), d. 1302. (27)
Linus. Greek poet. (4)
Loderingo. See Catalano. (23)
Lucy, Saint. An early Christian saint, patron saint of vision. (2)
Lucretia. Lucretia, wife of Collatine, was regarded by the Romans as a symbol of chaste uprightness, due to her suicide following her rape by the son of Tarquin. (4)
Manto. A witch, daughter of the prophet Tiresias. (20)
Martia. A woman of renown in Roman history; married to Cato of Utica. (4)
Maremma. See Corneto. (25, 29)
Menalippus. Tydeus, one of the seven kings who besieged Thebes, was mortally wounded as he killed the Theban warrior Menalippus. Tydeus demanded the head of his enemy and gnawed it in rage as he died. (32)
Michael (the Archangel). Chief among God's angelic host. (7)
Michael Scot. Philosopher, translator of the works of Aristotle, and student of the occult sciences, 1190-1250. (20)
Michel Zanche. Michel Zanche served as vicar to Enzio, king of Sardinia, and governed his provinces while Enzio was held prisoner by the Bolognese. Michel Zanche was murdered by his son-in-law Branca d'Oria, around 1290. (22, 33)
Mongibello. Mount Aetna, active volcano in Sicily, in mythology the site of the god Vulcan's forge. (14)
Montagna (de' Parcitati). See Romagna. (27)
Montaperti. A hill near Siena. (10)
Mordred. Nephew of King Arthur of Britain, Mordred attempted to usurp Arthur's throne, and Arthur killed him (receiving his own death wound in the process). Light was said to pass through the spear wound Arthur inflicted, which light interrupted the passage of Mordred's spirit. (32)
Mosca. A member of the Lamberti family of Florence, Mosca counseled the Uberti family to kill a certain Buondelmonte to avenge a broken engagement, with the line "What's done is finished." This resulted in bloody division of Florence into two feuding parties, the Guelphs and the Ghibellines. (6, 28)
Nasidius. In his *Pharsalia,* Lucan recounts the transformation into ashes of Cato's two soldiers Nasidius and Sabellus, when bitten by snakes. (25)
Nessus. See Dejanira. (12)

Niccolo (de' Salimbeni). A member of the Spendthrifts Club of Siena. (29)
Nisus. Trojan soldier, companion to Aeneas. (1)
Obizzo d'Este. A tyrant, Marquis of Ferrara. (12)
Orsini, "True son of the Orsini bear". Pope Nicholas III, Gian Gaetano degli Orsini, pope from 1277-1280. While pope he advanced many of his relatives (cubs) in ecclesiastical office. (19)
Penthesilea. The queen of the Amazons, she was the daughter of the god Mars. (4)
Pholus. A centaur who attempted the rape of Hippodamia during the brawl that accompanied her wedding. (12)
Photinus. A Thessalonican deacon. (11)
Piceno. See Pistoia. (24)
Piggy. This is Ciacco, a Florentine glutton. (6)
Pinamonte. See Casalodi. (20)
Pistoia. Vanni Fucci's prophecy: The Blacks of Pistoia, driven from the town in 1301, fled to Florence, which they then ruled, driving out members of the White party. Val di Magra belonged to Maroello Malaspina (lightning bolt) who led a force from Florence against Pistoia in 1302. The issue was joined at the battle of Serravalle, near Pistoia. (24)
Plutus. The god of wealth. (6, 7)
Polenta's eagle. See Romagna.
Polydorus. Son of king Priam of Troy, and of Hecuba. (30)
Polyxena. Daughter of Hecuba and king Priam of Troy. (30)
Prince of the new Pharisees. Pope Boniface VIII. See Boniface. (27)
Priscian. Latin grammarian, 6th century A. D. (15)
Ptolemy. Greek mathematician, first century A. D. (4)
Ptolemy's ice yard. This area of hell is named after the captain of Jericho (I *Maccabees)* who invited Simon and two of Simon's sons into his castle, and murdered them there. (33)
Puccio Sciancato (de Galigai). A Florentine thief. (25)
Pyrrhus. Perhaps the son of Achilles, who killed Priam and Priam's son Polites, and sacrificed Priam's daughter Polyxenes as well. It may also be Pyrrhus, king of Epirus, 318-372 B.C. (12)
Rinier da Corneto. A bandit. (12)
Rinier Pazzo. A bandit. (12)
Robert Guiscard. This Duke of Apulia and Calabria opposed the Greeks and Saracens in Sicily and southern Italy from 1059 until 1080. (28)
Romagna. The speaker who is identified as from Romagna (an Italian province between Bologna and the Adriatic) in the twenty-seventh canto, is Guido da Montefeltro, 1223-1298, the head of the Ghibellines of Romagna. His discourse with Dante generates, from Dante, the information that "Polenta's eagle" (Guido Minore, represented by his coat of arms) rules Ravenna; Sinibaldo degli Ordelaffi (the green lion) rules Forli; the castle of Verrucchio is controlled by Malatesta and his

son Malatestino of Rimini (the old mastiff and his pup), who gave "bad government" to Montagna de' Particati by taking him prisoner and killing him. (27)

Ruggieri (degli Ubaldini), Archbishop. See Ugolino. (33)

Sabellus. See Nasidius. (25)

Saint Peter's bronze pine cone. A huge pine cone, some seven feet high, and made of bronze, stood in front of St. Peter's in Rome in Dante's time. (31)

San Giovanni. The Baptistry in Florence. (19)

Sassol (Mascheroni). This member of the Toschi family of Florence killed either a nephew or a brother in order to obtain an inheritance. (32)

Semele. See Athamas. (30)

Sextus (Pompeius). The son of Pompey the Great, he was defeated at Munda by Julius Caesar in 45 B.C. (12)

Sichaeus. A Phoenecian, husband of Dido. (5)

Sicilian Bull. Perillus designed this instrument of torture for Phalaris, the tyrant of Sicily, and was required by his patron to test the machine himself. (27)

Sinon. The Greek who persuaded the Trojans to open their gates to the Trojan horse. (30)

Sismondi. Pisan family of the Ghibelline faction (33)

Stricca. A member of the Spendhrifts Brigade of Siena. (29)

Sylvester, (Pope I). The legend is that Sylvester, pope from 314-335, who had converted Constantine to Christianity, was summoned to cure him of leprosy. (27)

Tagliacozzo. See Alardo. (28)

Tebaldello. A member of the Zambrasi family of Faenze, he opened the gates of the city to allow entrance to enemies of the Lambertazzi family. (32)

Thames. "He in God's presence, let heart blood / that still is running into Thames." Guy de Montfort, in 1271, murdered Henry, nephew of the king of England, while Henry was at church in Viterbo. Henry's heart was returned to England in a casket, and placed in close proximity to the river Thames. (12)

Thibault. Teobaldo II (Thibaut V, Count of Champagne, King of Navarre, 1253-1270.) The man who identifies himself as having been king Thibault's domestic is given the name of Ciampolo. (22)

Traitor who sees out of one eye only. See Angiolello. (28)

Tydeus. One of the seven kings who besieges Thebes. (See Menalippus. (32)

Ubriachi. A Family of usurers from Florence. (17)

Ugolino. Count Ugolino, a Guelph, and Archbishop Ruggieri, the head of the Ghibelline party, both of Pisa, conspired together to expel Nino, Ugolino's grandson and political rival in his own party. That done, Ruggieri betrayed Ugolino, and imprisoned Ugolino and four of his sons and grandsons. The next year (1289), Guido da Montefeltro, taking control of the forces of Pisa, presided over the starvation of the captives. (33)

Ugo, "Little Ugo". Uguccione della Gherardesca, count Ugolino's son, and murdered with him. (33)

Vanni Fucci. Bastard son (mule) of Fuccio de' Lazzari of Pistoia, a thief. (24)

Venedico Caccianemico. See Ghisola. (18)

Verrucchio. See Romagna. (27)

Vicenza, Bishop of. Andrea dei Mozzi, Bishop of Florence from 1287-1295, and then translated by the pope (*"servus servorum"*) to the see of Vicenza. (15)

Vitaliano. Vitaliano de' Vitaliani, a usurer from Padua. The "most perfect knight" is Giovanni Buiamonte de' Bicci of Florence. (17)